WORKING
CAREER SUCCESS FOR THE 21st CENTURY
THIRD EDITION

Student Working Papers and Exploration Package

Larry J. Bailey
Professor
Workforce Education and
Development
Southern Illinois University
Carbondale, Illinois

THOMSON
™
SOUTH-WESTERN

Australia · Canada · Mexico · Singapore · Spain · United Kingdom · United States

THOMSON

SOUTH-WESTERN

Student Working Papers and Exploration Package
Working: Career Success for the 21st Century, 3d Edition
By Larry J. Bailey

Editor-in-Chief
Jack Calhoun

Vice President/Executive Publisher
Dave Shaut

Team Leader
Karen Schmohe

Acquisitions Editor
Joseph Vocca

Project Manager
Penny Shank

Consulting Editor
Elaine Langlois

Production Manager
Tricia Matthews Boies

Production Editor
Tim Bailey

Executive Marketing Manager
Carol Volz

Senior Marketing Manager
Nancy Long

Marketing Coordinator
Linda Kuper

Design Project Manager
Tippy McIntosh

Manufacturing Coordinator
Kevin Kluck

Editorial Assistant
Stephanie L. White

Production Assistant
Nancy Stamper

Cover Illustration
© Bek Shakirov/SIS

Cover and Internal Design
Bill Spencer

Printer
Globus Printing
Minster, Ohio

CONTENTS

PART 1

Chapter 1 Learning about Work 1
  1.1 Why People Work 2
  1.2 Occupations and Jobs, I 3
  1.3 Occupations and Jobs, II 4
  1.4 Training Agreement Responsibilities 5
  1.5 Benefits of Work Experience Education 6

Chapter 2 The Job Ahead 7
  2.1 About Work Histories 8
  2.2 Different Routes to a Stable Job 9
  2.3 Controlling Your Career 10

Chapter 3 Looking for a Job 11
  3.1 Clarifying Job Goals 12
  3.2 Application for a Social Security Number 13
  3.3 Sources of Job Leads 14
  3.4 Reading Help-wanted Ads 15
  3.5 Following Through 16

Chapter 4 Applying for a Job 17
  4.1 Job Application Documents and Methods 18
  4.2 Personal Data Sheet 19
  4.3 Job Application Form (Private Employer) 21
  4.4 Job Application Form (Government Employer) 23
  4.5 Resume 25
  4.6 Letter of Application 26
  4.7 Pre-employment Tests 27

Chapter 5 Interviewing for a Job 29
  5.1 Interviewer's Questions, I 30
  5.2 Interviewer's Questions, II 31
  5.3 Background Research 32
  5.4 Preparing for a Job Interview 33
  5.5 Follow-up Letter 34

Chapter 6 Beginning a New Job 35
  6.1 Organizational Structure 36
  6.2 Policies and Rules 37
  6.3 Completing a Form W-4 38
  6.4 Payroll Withholding 39
  6.5 Employment Terminology 40

Chapter 7 Expectations of Employers **41**
   7.1   Expectations of Employers 42
   7.2   Cost of Lost Production 43
   7.3   Rating Work Behavior 44

Chapter 8 Worker Rights and Protections **45**
   8.1   Worker Rights and Protections 46
   8.2   Equal Employment Opportunity 47
   8.3   Labor-Management Relations 48

Chapter 9 Human Relations at Work **49**
   9.1   Interpersonal Relations 50
   9.2   Customer Relations 51
   9.3   Working in Groups 53
   9.4   Special Human Relations Skills 54

Chapter 10 Earnings and Job Advancement **55**
   10.1   Your Paycheck 56
   10.2   Figuring Compensation 57
   10.3   Letter of Resignation 58

Chapter 11 Appearance on the Job **59**
   11.1   Personal Hygiene 60
   11.2   Hairstyling and Hair Care 61
   11.3   Dressing for the Job 62

Chapter 12 Career Decision Making **63**
   12.1   The Decision-making Process 64
   12.2   Decision-making Styles 65
   12.3   Influences on Decision Making 66

Chapter 13 Information About Your Self **67**
   13.1   Learning About Your Self 68
   13.2   Surveying Employees 69
   13.3   Rating Interests 70
   13.4   Rating Aptitudes 75
   13.5   Rating Work Values 77

Chapter 14 Career Information **79**
   14.1   Reading Tables and Charts 80
   14.2   Exploring Occupational Groups 81
   14.3   Using the *Occupational Outlook Handbook* 82
   14.4   Conducting an Occupational Search 83

Chapter 15 Communication Skills **85**
   15.1   Communication Skills 86
   15.2   Effective Listening 87
   15.3   Spelling and Grammar 88
   15.4   Correcting a Business Form 89
   15.5   Writing a Memo 90

Chapter 16 Math and Measurement Skills **91**
   16.1   Math and Measurement Terminology 92
   16.2   Basic Math 93
   16.3   Basic Measurement 95

Chapter 17 Safety Skills **97**
17.1   Preventing Accidents 98
17.2   Safety Practices Self-rating 99
17.3   Auto Safety Check Sheet 101
17.4   Safety Organizations 103

Chapter 18 Leadership Skills **105**
18.1   Leadership Characteristics 106
18.2   Career and Technical Student Organizations 107
18.3   Parliamentary Terms and Procedures 108

Chapter 19 Computer and Technology Skills **109**
19.1   Computer Literacy 110
19.2   Occupations and Computers 111
19.3   Robots 112
19.4   Working with Spreadsheets, I 113
19.5   Working with Spreadsheets, II 114

Chapter 20 Entrepreneurial Skills **115**
20.1   Advantages and Disadvantages of a Small Business 116
20.2   Interviewing an Entrepreneur 117
20.3   Entrepreneur Rating Scale 119
20.4   Planning for a Small Business 120

Chapter 21 Our Economic World **121**
21.1   Economics Terminology 122
21.2   Circular Flow of Economic Activity 123
21.3   Economic Growth 124

Chapter 22 The Consumer in the Marketplace **125**
22.1   Comparison Shopping 126
22.2   Advertising Techniques 127
22.3   Sales Come-ons 128
22.4   Used Car Prices 129
22.5   Letter of Complaint 130

Chapter 23 Banking and Credit **131**
23.1   Managing a Checking Account 132
23.2   Balancing a Bank Statement 134
23.3   The Cost of Credit 135
23.4   Credit Application 136

Chapter 24 Budgeting, Saving, and Investing Money **137**
24.1   Setting Financial Goals 138
24.2   Record of Income and Expenditures 139
24.3   Preparing a Budget 141
24.4   Selecting a Savings Account 142
24.5   Managing a Savings Account 143
24.6   Return on Savings and Investments 144

Chapter 25 Insuring Against Loss **145**
25.1   Insurance Protection 146
25.2   Which Type of Insurance? 148
25.3   Renter's Insurance 149
25.4   Automobile Insurance 150

Chapter 26 Taxes and Taxation **151**
   26.1   Tax Terminology 152
   26.2   Tax Rules 153
   26.3   Tax Rates 154
   26.4   Filing a Tax Return 155

Chapter 27 Social Security and IRAs **157**
   27.1   Social Security Coverage 158
   27.2   Administration and Financing of Social Security 159
   27.3   Individual Retirement Accounts 160

Chapter 28 The Legal System **161**
   28.1   The Nature of Law 162
   28.2   Types of Courts 163
   28.3   Small Claims Court 164

Chapter 29 Where to Live **165**
   29.1   Housing Needs and Wants 166
   29.2   Rental Agreement 167
   29.3   Tenant Relationships 169

Chapter 30 Healthful Living **171**
   30.1   Calorie Counting 172
   30.2   Calorie Expenditure 173
   30.3   Learning to Relax 174
   30.4   Healthstyle Self-rating 175
   30.5   Fitness Tests 177

Chapter 31 Responsible Citizenship **179**
   31.1   The Nature of Citizenship 180
   31.2   Elections and Voting 181
   31.3   Evaluating Propaganda 182

Chapter 32 Education for Lifelong Learning **183**
   32.1   Evaluating Educational Alternatives 184
   32.2   Seeking Educational Information 185
   32.3   Apprenticeship Interview 186

PART 2

Interpreting Information in the *OOH* 188

Sample Occupational Description 191

Managerial 194

Science and Technology 199

Human Services 205

Personal and Public Services 210

Health Services 214

Arts, Communications, and Entertainment 221

Business and Marketing 224

Mechanical 229

Construction 234

Production 238

Natural Resources 242

Military 244

Occupational Search Form 247

PART 1

ACTIVITIES

The activities that follow were developed to accompany the textbook *Working: Career Success for the 21st Century*. A total of 128 activities are included relating to the 32 textbook chapters. They provide opportunities for you to practice and apply concepts and skills introduced in the textbook.

A wide variety of problems, forms, rating scales, completion exercises, puzzles, and other approaches are used to make learning relevant and interesting. Some activities depend on use of the textbook. Others require you to use library or Internet reference materials or to collect information outside the school. A balance of individual- and group-oriented activities is provided. Most activities can be completed as part of a normal class period. A few activities, however, may require several days to complete.

In addition to reinforcing chapter objectives, these activities require you to apply communication, math and measurement, problem solving, and many other academic and employability skills. Some activities and exercises such as test-type items and math problems have only one correct answer. Many others, though, ask you to provide your own opinions and points of view. Do so. Think about the question and analyze the situation carefully before coming to a conclusion. Join with your classmates in follow-up discussion of the activities.

Work experience education has a very clear purpose: to help you obtain employment and succeed and progress on the job. The activities in this workbook can help you further develop the skills needed to progress toward a successful and satisfying career.

CHAPTER 1 Learning About Work

1.1 **Why People Work**
Objective: To become aware of the different reasons why people work

1.2 **Occupations and Jobs, I**
Objective: To recognize that a person having an occupation can work at many different jobs

1.3 **Occupations and Jobs, II**
Objective: To understand characteristics of jobs and occupations and their relationship

1.4 **Training Agreement Responsibilities**
Objective: To understand the responsibilities of the three parties involved in a training agreement

1.5 **Benefits of Work Experience Education**
Objective: To explain how selected individuals might benefit from work experience education

Name _____

Date _____

Select three employed individuals of different ages, sexes, and occupations. Show them the seven statements that follow. Have them rank the statements on scrap paper from most important (1) to least important (7). Then insert the rankings in this form. Combine the data with those of your classmates to compute an average for all the rankings. Complete the form and make a graph or chart of the results.

Reasons to Work	**1**	**2**	**3**	**Average**
■ Earn money	_____	_____	_____	_____
■ Be around people	_____	_____	_____	_____
■ It is satisfying and makes me feel good about myself.	_____	_____	_____	_____
■ Because people look up to me	_____	_____	_____	_____
■ To learn and grow	_____	_____	_____	_____
■ Makes me feel good physically	_____	_____	_____	_____
■ Allows me to express my interests and abilities	_____	_____	_____	_____

Study these data. What similarities and differences do you observe? _____

_____

_____

_____

_____

_____

_____

How do **your** reasons for wanting a job compare with the average rankings? _____

_____

_____

_____

_____

_____

Name _____

Date _____

A person having an occupation can work at many different types of jobs. For each occupation listed, identify three examples of different jobs where an individual could possibly work.

Auto mechanic

_____

_____

_____

Bookkeeper

_____

_____

_____

Child-care worker

_____

_____

_____

Data entry worker

_____

_____

_____

Dietician

_____

_____

_____

Drafter

_____

_____

_____

Laboratory technician

_____

_____

_____

Receptionist

_____

_____

_____

In the previous activity, you were asked to provide examples to illustrate how "a person having an occupation can work at many different types of jobs." Four additional characteristics about the relationship between occupations and jobs are stated below. Read each statement, study the example, and then complete the exercise.

1. A person may change jobs but keep the same occupation. For example, Ron was a welder at Deepwater Ship Building Company who left his job to work as a welder for High-Rise Construction Company. Provide another example of this relationship.

_____

_____

_____

2. A person may change occupations but keep the same job. For example, Lu-yin was a cashier at Town and Country Food Store. When the store expanded, Lu-yin was promoted to Assistant Store Manager. Provide another example of this relationship.

_____

_____

_____

3. A person may change both occupation and job. Gary was a medical laboratory technician at Metropolitan Hospital. He left this job to become a health occupations instructor at Lakeland Community College. Provide another example of this relationship.

_____

_____

_____

4. Persons having the same occupation may perform different duties on the job. For example, Tanya, who is a retail sales worker at Nadia's Dress Shop, spends most of her time at the cash register ringing up sales and bagging purchases. Lenoir, also a retail sales worker at Nadia's, spends most of her time assisting customers in the fitting room and marking garments for alterations. Provide another example of this relationship.

_____

_____

_____

■ Activity 1.4 Training Agreement
   Responsibilities

Name _____

Date _____

Work experience education involves a cooperative relationship among a student, a work experience teacher/coordinator, and an employer-supervisor. Each individual has different responsibilities. Study the training agreement used by your school or the one on page 10 of the textbook. Summarize the responsibilities of each party.

Student: _____

_____

_____

_____

Teacher/Coordinator: _____

_____

_____

_____

Employer-Supervisor: _____

_____

_____

_____

Who has the primary responsibility for making this three-way partnership work? _____

_____

_____

Who has the authority to terminate this agreement? _____

_____

_____

How will you be evaluated on the job? Discuss with your coordinator and supervisor

and summarize the process here. _____

_____

_____

_____

Explain how each of the following individuals might benefit from enrolling in a work experience education program.

1. Frank has completed one year of welding and is very good at it. But, because of the school's limited equipment, he cannot learn how to weld exotic metals such as monel, nickel, and titanium. He wants to enroll in a welding apprenticeship program after high school.

_____

_____

_____

2. Amy will be a senior in the fall, but she already has enough credits to graduate. She does not want to graduate early, however, because she participates in sports and does not want to miss the exciting senior year activities. She would not mind working one-half of the day.

_____

_____

_____

3. Seymour does not like any of his courses and his grades are poor. He is thinking about quitting school. What is the use in graduating, he wonders. Many of his friends are high school graduates and they cannot even get a job.

_____

_____

_____

4. Carmen is an above-average student who is thinking about attending a community college after graduation. She thinks she might prepare for a technical-level health occupation but is not sure. Her high school does not have any health occupations programs.

_____

_____

_____

CHAPTER 2 The Job Ahead

2.1 **About Work Histories**
Objective: To review what has been learned about work histories

2.2 **Different Routes to a Stable Job**
Objective: To recognize that individuals having different work histories can end up having the same or similar jobs

2.3 **Controlling Your Career**
Objective: To explain how various decisions, actions, and sacrifices might pay off later in a career

Knowing about different work histories can help you think about and plan for your own career. In Chapter 2 of the textbook (pages 18–19), review the sample work histories of **Terry**, **Marie**, **Cindy**, and **Rick**. State several helpful facts you learned from each of the cases.

Terry: _____

_____

_____

Marie: _____

_____

_____

Cindy: _____

_____

_____

Rick: _____

_____

_____

Answer the following questions about work histories by circling the letter T for each true statement and the letter F for each false statement.

T　　F　　1. Different work histories can lead to a stable job.

T　　F　　2. The best route to a stable job is to go to college directly after high school.

T　　F　　3. Jobs are often used as a way to achieve something else.

T　　F　　4. A stable job is one held at least ten years.

T　　F　　5. You may have a stable job at any time in your work life.

T　　F　　6. Advancing in a career sometimes involves taking risks.

T　　F　　7. Employers tend to recognize and reward good work.

T　　F　　8. It is better for a young person to hold off for a good job than to accept any job available.

T　　F　　9. Career preparation should include planning for change.

T　　F　　10. Most employers do not care about your school record.

Name _____

Date _____

Locate information in an encyclopedia or on the Web about the following recent Presidents of the United States. Summarize their work histories. Note that although their career patterns are quite different, all the men ended up with the same job.

George W. Bush _____

_____

_____

_____

_____

_____

_____

Bill Clinton _____

_____   President
of the
United
States
_____

_____

_____

_____

_____

George Bush _____

_____

_____

_____

_____

_____

_____

■ Activity 2.3 Controlling Your Career

Name _____

Date _____

Explain how the following decisions, actions, and sacrifices might pay off later.

1. Attending a local community college rather than a four-year university because that is all you can afford _____

   _____

   _____

2. Accepting a temporary or part-time job even though you would like to have a full-time, permanent position _____

   _____

   _____

3. Willingly staying after work an extra hour without pay to help finish up an important assignment _____

   _____

   _____

4. Taking pride in what you are doing and giving the job your best effort _____

   _____

   _____

5. Taking an evening course to learn a new skill _____

   _____

   _____

6. Working evenings and weekends to earn money for college, even though you would rather be out with your friends _____

   _____

   _____

7. Reducing the number of hours worked each week to devote more time to schoolwork

   _____

   _____

CHAPTER 3 Looking for a Job

3.1 **Clarifying Job Goals**
Objective: To think about and clarify job goals

3.2 **Application for a Social Security Number**
Objective: To practice filling out an application form

3.3 **Sources of Job Leads**
Objective: To identify specific job leads associated with various sources

3.4 **Reading Help-wanted Ads**
Objective: To learn common abbreviations found in help-wanted ads

3.5 **Following Through**
Objective: To give recommendations for following through on job leads in various situations

Name _____

Date _____

The benefits of work experience education can help you to clarify your own job goals. Which of the following benefits are most important to you? Rank them from high (1) to low (7).

Benefits	**Rank**
■ Learn occupational skills	_____
■ Develop employability skills	_____
■ Establish a work record	_____
■ Earn while you learn	_____
■ Discover career interests and goals	_____
■ Recognize the relationship between education and work	_____
■ Remain employed after graduation	_____

You will probably be asked the following question many times: "Why do you want a job?" Think about the question and write your answer.

_____

_____

_____

_____

_____

_____

_____

_____

_____

_____

_____

_____

_____

_____

Prepare to apply for a Social Security number by filling out the sample application that follows.

SOCIAL SECURITY ADMINISTRATION
Application for a Social Security Card

Form Approved
OMB No. 0960-0066

		First	Full Middle Name	Last
1	**NAME** ➡️ TO BE SHOWN ON CARD			
	FULL NAME AT BIRTH IF OTHER THAN ABOVE	First	Full Middle Name	Last
	OTHER NAMES USED			

		Street Address, Apt. No., PO Box, Rural Route No.		
2	**MAILING ADDRESS** Do Not Abbreviate			
		City	State	Zip Code

3 **CITIZENSHIP** ➡️ (Check One)
☐ U.S. Citizen   ☐ Legal Alien Allowed To Work   ☐ Legal Alien **Not** Allowed To Work (See Instructions On Page 1)   ☐ Other (See Instructions On Page 1)

4 **SEX** ➡️   ☐ Male   ☐ Female

5 **RACE/ETHNIC DESCRIPTION** (Check One Only - Voluntary) ➡️
☐ Asian, Asian-American or Pacific Islander   ☐ Hispanic   ☐ Black (Not Hispanic)   ☐ North American Indian or Alaskan Native   ☐ White (Not Hispanic)

6 **DATE OF BIRTH** (Month, Day, Year)   **7** **PLACE OF BIRTH** (Do Not Abbreviate)   City   State or Foreign Country   FCI   Office Use Only

		First	Full Middle Name	Last Name At Her Birth
8	**A. MOTHER'S MAIDEN NAME** ➡️			
	B. MOTHER'S SOCIAL SECURITY NUMBER ➡️	☐☐☐ – ☐☐ – ☐☐☐☐		

		First	Full Middle Name	Last
9	**A. FATHER'S NAME** ➡️			
	B. FATHER'S SOCIAL SECURITY NUMBER ➡️	☐☐☐ – ☐☐ – ☐☐☐☐		

10 Has the applicant or anyone acting on his/her behalf ever filed for or received a Social Security number card before?
☐ Yes (If "yes", answer questions 11-13.)   ☐ No (If "no", go on to question 14.)   ☐ Don't Know (If "don't know", go on to question 14.)

11 Enter the Social Security number previously assigned to the person listed in item 1. ➡️   ☐☐☐ – ☐☐ – ☐☐☐☐

12 Enter the name shown on the most recent Social Security card issued for the person listed in item 1. ➡️   First   Middle Name   Last

13 Enter any different date of birth if used on an earlier application for a card. ➡️   Month, Day, Year

14 **TODAY'S DATE** Month, Day, Year   **15** **DAYTIME PHONE NUMBER** ( ) Area Code   Number

DELIBERATELY FURNISHING (OR CAUSING TO BE FURNISHED) FALSE INFORMATION ON THIS APPLICATION IS A CRIME PUNISHABLE BY FINE OR IMPRISONMENT, OR BOTH.

16 **YOUR SIGNATURE** ▶   **17** **YOUR RELATIONSHIP TO THE PERSON IN ITEM 1 IS:**
☐ Self   ☐ Natural Or Adoptive Parent   ☐ Legal Guardian   ☐ Other (Specify)

DO NOT WRITE BELOW THIS LINE (FOR SSA USE ONLY)

NPN			DOC	NTI	CAN		ITV
PBC	EVI	EVA	EVC	PRA	NWR	DNR	UNIT

EVIDENCE SUBMITTED

SIGNATURE AND TITLE OF EMPLOYEE(S) REVIEWING EVIDENCE AND/OR CONDUCTING INTERVIEW

DATE

DCL   DATE

Form **SS-5** (3-2001) EF (3-2001) Destroy Prior Editions Page 5

Name _____

Date _____

The most common sources of job leads are listed. Consult each source and try to write down at least one lead. Check off (✓) each source after you have made the contact(s).

(✓)

_____ Relatives

_____

_____

_____ Neighbors

_____

_____

_____ Friends

_____

_____

_____ Work experience coordinator

_____

_____

_____ Guidance counselor

_____

_____

_____ School placement officer

_____

_____

_____ Help-wanted ads

_____

_____

_____ Job Service

_____

_____

_____ Private employment agency

_____

_____

_____ Employer contact

_____

_____

_____ Telephone Yellow Pages

_____

_____

_____ Internet

_____

_____

Name _____

Date _____

Abbreviations are often used in help-wanted ads to save space. The following are a number of abbreviations found in newspaper classified ads. Write out the meaning of each.

appt _____   hvy equip _____

ASAP _____   info _____

ass't _____   lic'd _____

avail _____   M/F/D/V _____

CRT _____   mfg _____

deg _____   mgr _____

EDP _____   OTR drive _____

EOE _____   ref _____

eves & wknds _____   req'd _____

exp pref'd _____   sales rep _____

flex hrs _____   sal neg _____

fringes _____   temp _____

f/time _____   trng _____

hrly _____   WPM _____

Look at the help-wanted ads in a newspaper and see if you can identify additional abbreviations not listed. Write the abbreviations and their meaning on the lines that follow.

_____   _____

_____   _____

_____   _____

_____   _____

_____   _____

_____   _____

For each of these situations, write down what the person could do to follow through and try to get a job.

1. Alberto learns from his guidance counselor about a good position. It is the last day to apply. He gets himself ready and drives to the business. The receptionist is not very helpful. She tells Alberto that she is a temporary employee and is not sure whom to call. She is quite busy.

   _____

   _____

   _____

2. On Saturday, Sarah learns from a friend that her mother is looking for immediate help in her day-care center and has placed an ad in the Sunday paper. It is exactly the kind of job that Sarah wants.

   _____

   _____

   _____

3. David is passing by a sandwich shop when he sees a help-wanted sign in the front window. When he walks in, he finds that there are six people ahead of him, all applying for the same job. David wonders whether it is worth applying or whether he should come back later.

   _____

   _____

4. Late one afternoon, Mei-ling sees a posting at her school placement office for an assistant at a pet store. She knows the pet store and would like to work there. It is the last day for receiving applications. The ad says to apply in writing.

   _____

   _____

5. Tina's sister is leaving her job at a clothing shop at the mall to return to college. She mentions to Tina that a lot of jobs will be opening up at the mall with college students going back to school.

   _____

   _____

   _____

CHAPTER 4 Applying for a Job

4.1 **Job Application Documents and Methods**
Objective: To review characteristics of documents and methods used to apply for a job

4.2 **Personal Data Sheet**
Objective: To prepare a personal data sheet

4.3 **Job Application Form (Private Employer)**
Objective: To practice filling out a job application form

4.4 **Job Application Form (Government Employer)**
Objective: To practice filling out a job application form

4.5 **Resume**
Objective: To prepare a job resume

4.6 **Letter of Application**
Objective: To write a sample letter of application

4.7 **Pre-employment Tests**
Objective: To become familiar with the nature of a general ability test

Name _____

Date _____

Test your knowledge of the types of documents and methods used to apply for a job by completing the following two exercises.

Match the document (a, b, or c) with the statement below that best describes it.

a. Personal data sheet
b. Job application form
c. Resume

_____ 1. Helps employers screen applicants for interviews.

_____ 2. Contains a short statement of career goals.

_____ 3. Contains complete, detailed information, even though some data may not always be used.

_____ 4. Sent with a cover letter when applying for a job by mail.

_____ 5. Should be checked carefully before mailing or giving to an employer.

_____ 6. Never given directly to an employer.

_____ 7. Provides job seekers with information normally required by employers.

_____ 8. Usually limited to one page.

_____ 9. First of the three types of documents to be completed.

_____ 10. May be brief or quite detailed.

Match the job application method (a, b, c, or d) with the statement below that best describes it.

a. Applying in person
b. Applying by telephone
c. Applying in writing (letter of application)
d. Applying online

_____ 11. A job seeker can make more contacts in less time this way.

_____ 12. This is similar to going for a job interview.

_____ 13. Its purpose is to attract and hold an employer's interest.

_____ 14. It is important to be organized before contacting an employer this way.

_____ 15. Good verbal skills are important with this method.

_____ 16. This method also calls attention to the resume.

_____ 17. For this method, you may use keywords relating to the position you want.

_____ 18. First impressions are important with this method.

_____ 19. This kind of application may be made in several ways.

_____ 20. This may result in the immediate need to complete a job application form.

A personal data sheet is useful in completing job application forms and in developing a resume. Complete the following form by filling in each item that applies to you.

PERSONAL DATA SHEET

IDENTIFICATION

Name _____ Soc. Sec. # _____

Address _____

Telephone (___) _____

E-mail Address _____

Hobbies/Interests _____

Honors/Awards/Offices _____

Sports/Activities _____

Other _____

EDUCATIONAL BACKGROUND

School Name and Address	Dates Attended	
	From:	To:
High School:		
Course of Study _____ Rank _____	GPA _____	
Favorite Subject(s) _____		
Other (College, Trade, Business, or Correspondence School):	From:	To:
Course of Study _____ Rank _____	GPA _____	
Favorite Subject(s) _____		
Other (College, Trade, Business, or Correspondence School):	From:	To:
Course of Study _____ Rank _____	GPA _____	
Favorite Subject(s) _____		

(Continued on next page)

Name _____

Date _____

EMPLOYMENT HISTORY

(Start with present or most recent employer.)

1. Company _____ Telephone (___) _____

Address _____

Employed from Mo. _____ Yr. _____ /to Mo. _____ Yr. _____ Supervisor _____

Position/Title _____

Last Wage _____ Reason for Leaving _____

2. Company _____ Telephone (___) _____

Address _____

Employed from Mo. _____ Yr. _____ /to Mo. _____ Yr. _____ Supervisor _____

Position/Title _____

Last Wage _____ Reason for Leaving _____

3. Company _____ Telephone (___) _____

Address _____

Employed from Mo. _____ Yr. _____ /to Mo. _____ Yr. _____ Supervisor _____

Position/Title _____

Last Wage _____ Reason for Leaving _____

REFERENCES

1. Name _____ Title _____

Address _____

Relationship _____ Telephone (___) _____

2. Name _____ Title _____

Address _____

Relationship _____ Telephone (___) _____

3. Name _____ Title _____

Address _____

Relationship _____ Telephone (___) _____

■ **Activity 4.3 Job Application Form (Private Employer)**

Name _____

Date _____

Prepare to complete a job application form by filling out the following sample. Use the personal data sheet you completed in the previous activity.

EMPLOYMENT APPLICATION

This company is an equal opportunity employer and does not discriminate in hiring or in terms or conditions of employment because of race, color, creed, religion, national origin, sex, age, or disability. This company only hires individuals authorized for employment in the United States.

Position applying for: _____ Today's date: _____

Schedule desired: ( ) Full-time ( ) Temporary ( ) Part-time   Salary required: _____

PERSONAL INFORMATION

Name: _____

Address: _____
          Street   City   State   ZIP

How long have you lived there (years/months)? _____ / _____   Phone: _____
                                                Years   Months

Previous address: _____
                    Street   City   State   ZIP

How long did you live there (years/months)? _____ / _____   Phone: _____
                                             Years   Months

Age (if under 18): _____ Social Security number: _____

Are you authorized for employment in the United States? ( ) Yes   ( ) No

EDUCATION

High school: _____
              Name   City   State

Degree/area of study: _____ Years attended:_____Graduated? ( ) Yes ( ) No

College: _____
          Name   City   State

Degree/area of study: _____ Years attended:_____Graduated? ( ) Yes ( ) No

Graduate school: _____
                  Name   City   State

Degree/area of study: _____ Years attended:_____Graduated? ( ) Yes ( ) No

Other: _____
        Name   City   State

Degree/area of study: _____ Years attended:_____Graduated? ( ) Yes ( ) No

SKILLS

Describe skills relevant to the position applied for: _____

_____

(Continued on next page)

EMPLOYMENT HISTORY

List employment starting with your most recent position. Continue on a separate page as needed. Account for any time during this period that you were unemployed on a separate page. If you have fewer than three places of employment, please provide three personal references on a separate page.

May we contact your present employer? ( ) Yes ( ) No

Employer: _____
         Name   Street

City   State   ZIP   Phone   E-mail
Job title: _____Responsibilities: _____

Start date: _____ End date: _____ Supervisor: _____

Starting wage: _____ Final wage: _____ Reason for leaving: _____

Employer: _____
         Name   Street

City   State   ZIP   Phone   E-mail
Job title: _____Responsibilities: _____

Start date: _____ End date: _____ Supervisor: _____

Starting wage: _____ Final wage: _____ Reason for leaving: _____

Employer: _____
         Name   Street

City   State   ZIP   Phone   E-mail
Job title: _____Responsibilities: _____

Start date: _____ End date: _____ Supervisor: _____

Starting wage: _____ Final wage: _____ Reason for leaving: _____

MISCELLANEOUS

Have you been employed by this company before? ( ) Yes ( ) No   If you answered yes, please indicate dates and positions: _____

List relatives or acquaintances employed by this company: _____

Have you ever been convicted of a crime? ( ) Yes ( ) No   If you answered yes, please explain: _____

I hereby affirm that the information I have given on this application is complete and accurate. I understand that any falsification or omission will be grounds for immediate dismissal. I authorize a thorough investigation in connection with this application and authorize the release of documents and personal interviews with third parties, such as prior employers, family members, and business associates. If hired, I agree that my employment and compensation can be terminated without cause or notice at any time at the option of the company or myself. I understand that no representative of the company, other than a Vice President, has the authority to enter into any agreement for employment for any specified period of time or to make any agreement contrary to the foregoing.

Signature _____   Date _____

This is a typical form used in hiring various civil service classifications. Complete the form by filling in each item that applies to you.

APPLICATION FOR CIVIL SERVICE EMPLOYMENT

Last Name _____ First Name _____ Middle Name _____

Address _____

City _____ State _____ ZIP _____ County _____

Home Phone _____ Work Phone _____

Social Security Number _____ Age (if under 18) _____

If applying for a **vacant position,** fill in the information below:

Job title _____ Position Control No. (PCN) _____ Deadline _____

If applying for a **civil service examination,** fill in the information below.

Exam Title _____ Exam No. _____ Deadline _____

Type of work desired: _____ ☐ Full-time ☐ Part-time

1. Do you claim veterans' preference? ☐ Yes ☐ No
2. Have you ever been a state or county employee? ☐ Yes ☐ No
   If you are currently a state employee: Job Title _____ Job No. _____
3. Have you ever been convicted of a felony? ☐ Yes ☐ No
   A felony conviction will not necessarily be a bar to employment.
4. Have you ever been suspended or discharged from any position? ☐ Yes ☐ No

If you answered yes to Question 2, 3, or 4, please explain fully. _____

_____

LICENSES, REGISTRATIONS, AND CERTIFICATES

Be sure to include any valid drivers license or commercial drivers license if required for the job.

Issued by	Field/Trade/Specialization	License/Certificate No.	Expires

EDUCATION

Circle highest grade completed   1   2   3   4   5   6   7   8   9   10   11   12   GED

Circle full academic year of college completed   1   2   3   4   5   6   7   8

Are you currently attending school (for intern positions)? ☐ Yes ☐ No   Level _____

List schools attended after high school. Include technical, business, and professional schools and colleges.

School Name and Location	Major Area(s) of Study	Degree or Certification

(Continued on next page)

List any relevant course work you have taken at the high school level or beyond relevant to the position or examination for which you are applying.

TRAINING AND OTHER QUALIFICATIONS

Subject or Title	Organization	Length of Training

List special equipment or machines you can operate. _____

_____

List computer software in which you have skill, including word processing, spreadsheet, and database programs. Please indicate the name of the specific software. _____

_____

List special clerical skills, including keying and shorthand._____

_____Keying speed:_____

List any additional relevant skills you have. _____

_____

List your past work experience beginning with your most recent employment. Use additional sheets if necessary.

Name, address, and phone number of employing firm _____

_____Dates_____

Supervisor _____Job title _____Reason for leaving_____

Salary _____Description of work _____

Name, address, and phone number of employing firm _____

_____Dates_____

Supervisor _____Job title _____Reason for leaving_____

Salary _____Description of work _____

Name, address, and phone number of employing firm _____

_____Dates_____

Supervisor _____Job title _____Reason for leaving_____

Salary _____Description of work _____

Name, address, and phone number of employing firm _____

_____Dates_____

Supervisor _____Job title _____Reason for leaving_____

Salary _____Description of work _____

I certify that the information I have supplied in this application is true and complete to the best of my knowledge. I understand that if this application is not completed in full, it will not be processed and I will be disqualified. I understand that a background check may be required prior to employment and that drug testing may be required. I consent that my past employers may disclose any information relevant to my employment to the agency to which I am applying. I understand that any offer of employment is contingent upon proof of legal authorization to work in the United States as required by the Immigration Reform and Control Act.

Signature _____Date _____

Name _____

Date _____

Prepare a draft of a resume by following the outline below. Refer to your personal data sheet as necessary. After your instructor has reviewed your draft, key your resume, proofread it, and make any corrections that are needed. Then have your resume duplicated for distribution to potential employers. Do not exceed one page.

_____

_____

_____

_____

CAREER GOALS: _____

_____

_____

EDUCATIONAL BACKGROUND: _____

_____

_____

_____

_____

WORK EXPERIENCE: _____

_____

_____

_____

_____

REFERENCES:

_____ _____

_____ _____

_____ _____

_____ _____

_____ _____

Name _____

Date _____

Write a draft of a letter applying for a real or hypothetical job. Follow the four guidelines on page 54 of your text. After the letter has been reviewed by your instructor, format it correctly, key it neatly, and proofread it as discussed on page 54 and illustrated on page 55.

_____

_____

_____

_____

_____

_____

_____

Dear _____

_____

_____

_____

_____

_____

_____

_____

_____

_____

_____

_____

_____

Sincerely

_____

Enclosure

■ Activity 4.7 Pre-employment Tests

Name _____

Date _____

One type of pre-employment test is a general ability test. This type of test measures basic academic knowledge and skills. Answer the following questions and you will have an idea of what such tests are like.

General Science

1. An eclipse of the sun throws the shadow of the

   a. moon on the sun.
   b. moon on the earth.
   c. earth on the sun.
   d. earth on the moon.

2. Substances that hasten chemical reaction time without themselves undergoing change are called

   a. buffers.
   b. colloids.
   c. reducers.
   d. catalysts.

Word Knowledge

3. If the wind is *variable* today, that means it is

   a. mild.
   b. steady.
   c. shifting.
   d. chilling.

4. *Rudiments* most nearly means

   a. politics.
   b. minute details.
   c. promotion opportunities.
   d. basic methods and procedures.

Understanding Paragraphs

5. Twenty-five percent of all household burglaries can be attributed to unlocked windows or doors. Crime is the result of opportunity plus desire. To prevent crime, each individual has the responsibility to

   a. provide the desire.
   b. provide the opportunity.
   c. prevent the desire.
   d. prevent the opportunity.

Math Knowledge

6. If x + 6 = 7, what does x equal?

   a. 0
   b. 1
   c. −1
   d. $^7/_8$

7. What is the area of this square?

   a. 1 square foot
   b. 5 square feet
   c. 10 square feet
   d. 25 square feet

5 FT.

(Continued on next page)

Name _____

Date _____

Math Reasoning

8. How many 36-passenger buses would it take to carry 144 people?

   a. 3
   b. 4
   c. 5
   d. 6

9. It costs $0.50 per square yard to waterproof canvas. What will it cost to waterproof a canvas truck cover that is 15' x 24'?

   a. $6.67
   b. $18.00
   c. $20.00
   d. $180.00

Mechanical Knowledge

10. Which post holds up the greater part of the load?

    a. Post A
    b. Post B
    c. both equal
    d. not clear

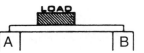

11. In this arrangement of pulleys, which pulley turns fastest?

    a. A
    b. B
    c. C
    d. D

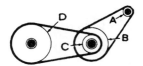

Electronics Information

12. Which of the following has the least resistance?

    a. wood
    b. iron
    c. rubber
    d. silver

13. In this circuit diagram, the resistance is 100 ohms and the current is 0.1 amperes. The voltage is

    a. 5 volts.
    b. 10 volts.
    c. 100 volts.
    d. 1,000 volts.

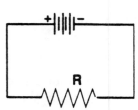

Auto and Shop Information

14. A car uses too much oil when which parts are worn?

    a. pistons
    b. piston rings
    c. main bearings
    d. connecting rods

15. The saw shown below is used mainly to cut

    a. plywood.
    b. odd-shaped holes in wood.
    c. along the grain of the wood.
    d. across the grain of the wood.

Reproduced from *ASVAB 18/19 Counselor Manual*, July 1992

CHAPTER 5 Interviewing for a Job

5.1 Interviewer's Questions, I
Objective: To prepare responses to standard questions asked at a job interview

5.2 Interviewer's Questions, II
Objective: To prepare responses to potential interview questions related to a specific company and job

5.3 Background Research
Objective: To learn about the work performed in various types of companies

5.4 Preparing for a Job Interview
Objective: To develop sample questions and comments in preparation for a job interview

5.5 Follow-up Letter
Objective: To practice writing a follow-up letter

Name _____

Date _____

Even though an interviewer will probably look over your job application form and resume in advance, he or she may still ask a number of basic questions. Be prepared by thinking about and writing an answer to the following questions:

1. Tell me something about yourself. _____

_____

_____

2. What type of work do your parents or family do? _____

_____

_____

3. What are your best and worst subjects in school? _____

_____

_____

4. What do you like to do in your spare time? _____

_____

_____

5. If I called one of the persons you listed as a reference, what do you think he or she would

say about you? _____

_____

_____

6. What types of previous jobs have you held? _____

_____

_____

7. Were you ever fired from a previous job? If so, why? _____

_____

_____

8. What do you want to be doing five years from now? _____

_____

_____

Name _____

Date _____

In addition to basic questions such as those in the previous activity, an interviewer may ask more specific questions about you and the job you are interested in. Name a company and a job you are applying for and then answer the following questions in relation to them.

Company_____ Job Title_____

1. Why did you apply for a job with us? _____

_____

_____

2. What do you know about the type of work we do here? _____

_____

_____

3. Why do you think you would like this type of work? _____

_____

_____

4. What specific job skills do you have? _____

_____

_____

5. If I hired you, how long would you expect to stay with us? _____

_____

_____

6. How much would you expect to be paid? _____

_____

_____

7. I have a number of qualified applicants for this job. Why should I hire you? _____

_____

_____

8. What questions would you like to ask me? _____

_____

_____

■ **Activity 5.3 Background Research**

Name _____

Date _____

Before going to a job interview, you should learn something about the type of industry in which the job is located. Use the *Standard Industrial Classification Manual* (available as "SIC Manual" at ***http://www.osha.gov/***), the newer *North American Industry Classification Manual*, an encyclopedia, the Web, or another source to locate information about the companies.

1. Aluminum smelter: _____

_____

2. Boiler shop: _____

_____

3. Commodity broker: _____

_____

4. Freight forwarding company: _____

_____

5. Holding company: _____

_____

6. Limestone quarry: _____

_____

7. Lumber jobber: _____

_____

8. Lithographic printer: _____

_____

9. News syndicate: _____

_____

10. Ornamental floriculturist: _____

_____

11. Outpatient care facility: _____

_____

12. Operative builder: _____

_____

Date _____

A job interview involves two-way communications. Identify a job that you would like to have. List five questions that you might want to ask the interviewer.

Job: _____

_____

1. _____

_____

2. _____

_____

3. _____

_____

4. _____

_____

5. _____

_____

Many job applicants fail to ask for the job. Before you leave the interview, tell the interviewer if you want the job. Provide an example here of what you might say:

_____

_____

_____

_____

Assume that the interviewer offers you the job. List below any questions you might ask or statements you might make before accepting or rejecting the job.

_____

_____

_____

_____

Assume that you have had an interview with Ms. Karen Judkins, Personnel Manager of the Ozark State Bank, for a job as a teller. She will not make a decision for about a week, until several other applicants have been interviewed. You would like to have the job. Write a draft of an appropriate follow-up letter. Follow the guidelines on pages 71 and 72 of the text. The bank's address is 14 Main St., Leslie, AR 72465-1105.

_____

_____

_____

_____

_____

_____

Dear _____

_____

_____

_____

_____

_____

_____

_____

_____

_____

_____

Sincerely

_____

CHAPTER 6 Beginning a New Job

6.1 **Organizational Structure**
Objective: To develop a relevant organizational chart and to understand its function within the organization

6.2 **Policies and Rules**
Objective: To explain the underlying rationale for various workplace policies and rules

6.3 **Completing a Form W-4**
Objective: To learn how to fill out a Form W-4

6.4 **Payroll Withholding**
Objective: To recognize the basis by which an employer deducts an amount for federal income tax

6.5 **Employment Terminology**
Objective: To become familiar with terms that new employees are likely to encounter

■ **Activity 6.1 Organizational Structure**   Name _____

Date _____

Diagram the organizational structure for the company in which you are employed. If you do not have a job, use your school system.

Draw an arrow to indicate your position in the organization. Describe the chain of command that you would follow if you wanted to pursue a complaint to the highest level of authority in the organization. Also, draw this path in your figure using a colored marking pen or highlighter.

_____

_____

_____

_____

_____

_____

_____

The following are a number of typical statements found in a company policy manual. Assume that you are the employer. Explain the reason for each policy or rule.

1. Each employee must punch his or her own time card when beginning or ending work.

   _____

   _____

2. An employee is docked 15 minutes' pay for each quarter-hour period in which he or she is late. (For example, a person who clocks in at 7:03 is figured for payroll purposes as having started work at 7:15.)

   _____

   _____

3. If you are ill or cannot come to work, notify your immediate supervisor as early as possible, but no later than the scheduled starting time for your shift.

   _____

   _____

4. Company supplies, tools, or equipment may not be removed from company premises. Employees found in violation of this rule face disciplinary action or possible termination.

   _____

   _____

5. Local personal phone calls during working hours should be kept to a minimum. Long-distance personal calls charged to the company are prohibited.

   _____

   _____

6. Each employee who has completed the probationary period is eligible for two weeks (ten days) of paid vacation. The vacation period must be requested through and approved by your immediate supervisor.

   _____

   _____

7. Two-week written notification is required for voluntarily terminating employment. Submit a letter to your immediate supervisor.

   _____

   _____

Name _____

Date _____

One of the first things you will do after being hired is to complete a Form W-4. The information you provide on the form will be used by the employer to withhold the correct amount of federal income tax from your paycheck. Learn how to complete the form by filling out the Personal Allowances Worksheet and practice Form W-4 below. Your instructor will provide additional information regarding line E and any other worksheets that might apply.

Personal Allowances Worksheet (Keep for your records.)

A Enter "1" for **yourself** if no one else can claim you as a dependent . . . . **A** _____

B Enter "1" if:
- You are single and have only one job; or
- You are married, have only one job, and your spouse does not work; or
- Your wages from a second job or your spouse's wages (or the total of both) are $1,000 or less.

. . **B** _____

C Enter "1" for your **spouse**. But, you may choose to enter "-0-" if you are married and have either a working spouse or more than one job. (Entering "-0-" may help you avoid having too little tax withheld.). . . . . **C** _____

D Enter number of **dependents** (other than your spouse or yourself) you will claim on your tax return . . . . **D** _____

E Enter "1" if you will file as **head of household** on your tax return (see conditions under **Head of household** above) . **E** _____

F Enter "1" if you have at least $1,500 of **child or dependent care expenses** for which you plan to claim a credit . . **F** _____

(**Note:** Do **not** include child support payments. See **Pub. 503,** Child and Dependent Care Expenses, for details.)

G **Child Tax Credit** (including additional child tax credit):
- If your total income will be between $15,000 and $42,000 ($20,000 and $65,000 if married), enter "1" for each eligible child plus **1 additional** if you have three to five eligible children or **2 additional** if you have six or more eligible children.
- If your total income will be between $42,000 and $80,000 ($65,000 and $115,000 if married), enter "1" if you have one or two eligible children, "2" if you have three eligible children, "3" if you have four eligible children, or "4" if you have five or more eligible children. **G** _____

H Add lines A through G and enter total here. **Note:** This may be different from the number of exemptions you claim on your tax return. ▶ **H** _____

For accuracy, complete all worksheets that apply.
- If you plan to **itemize or claim adjustments to income** and want to reduce your withholding, see the **Deductions and Adjustments Worksheet** on page 2.
- If you have **more than one job** or are **married and you and your spouse both work** and the combined earnings from all jobs exceed $35,000, see the **Two-Earner/Two-Job Worksheet** on page 2 to avoid having too little tax withheld.
- If **neither** of the above situations applies, **stop here** and enter the number from line H on line 5 of Form W-4 below.

- - - - - - - - - - - - - - - **Cut here and give Form W-4 to your employer. Keep the top part for your records.** - - - - - - - - - - - - - - -

Form **W-4** Department of the Treasury Internal Revenue Service	**Employee's Withholding Allowance Certificate** ▶ **For Privacy Act and Paperwork Reduction Act Notice, see page 2.**	OMB No. 1545-0010 20**02**

1 Type or print your first name and middle initial Last name	**2** Your social security number

Home address (number and street or rural route)	**3** ☐ Single ☐ Married ☐ Married, but withhold at higher Single rate. **Note:** If married, but legally separated, or spouse is a nonresident alien, check the "Single" box.
City or town, state, and ZIP code	**4** If your last name differs from that on your social security card, check here. You must call 1-800-772-1213 for a new card. ▶ ☐

5 Total number of allowances you are claiming (from line **H** above **or** from the applicable worksheet on page 2) **5** _____

6 Additional amount, if any, you want withheld from each paycheck . . . . **6** $ _____

7 I claim exemption from withholding for 2002, and I certify that I meet **both** of the following conditions for exemption:
- Last year I had a right to a refund of **all** Federal income tax withheld because I had **no** tax liability **and**
- This year I expect a refund of **all** Federal income tax withheld because I expect to have **no** tax liability.
If you meet both conditions, write "Exempt" here . . . . ▶ **7** _____

Under penalties of perjury, I certify that I am entitled to the number of withholding allowances claimed on this certificate, or I am entitled to claim exempt status.

Employee's signature (Form is not valid unless you sign it.) ▶ _____ Date ▶ _____

8 Employer's name and address (Employer: Complete lines 8 and 10 only if sending to the IRS.)	**9** Office code (optional)	**10** Employer identification number

Cat. No. 10220Q

Name _____

Date _____

The following is part of the table an employer uses to figure the amount of income tax to be withheld from the weekly paycheck of a single person. Use the chart as required to answer the questions that follow.

SINGLE Persons—WEEKLY Payroll Period
(For Wages Paid in 2002)

If the wages are—		And the number of withholding allowances claimed is—										
At least	But less than	0	1	2	3	4	5	6	7	8	9	10
		The amount of income tax to be withheld is—										
195	200	16	9	3	0	0	0	0	0	0	0	0
200	210	17	10	4	0	0	0	0	0	0	0	0
210	220	19	11	5	0	0	0	0	0	0	0	0
220	230	20	12	6	0	0	0	0	0	0	0	0
230	240	22	13	7	1	0	0	0	0	0	0	0
240	250	23	15	8	2	0	0	0	0	0	0	0
250	260	25	16	9	3	0	0	0	0	0	0	0
260	270	26	18	10	4	0	0	0	0	0	0	0
270	280	28	19	11	5	0	0	0	0	0	0	0
280	290	29	21	12	6	0	0	0	0	0	0	0
290	300	31	22	14	7	1	0	0	0	0	0	0
300	310	32	24	15	8	2	0	0	0	0	0	0
310	320	34	25	17	9	3	0	0	0	0	0	0
320	330	35	27	18	10	4	0	0	0	0	0	0
330	340	37	28	20	11	5	0	0	0	0	0	0
340	350	38	30	21	12	6	1	0	0	0	0	0

1. How much income tax should be withheld for the following individuals?

   $225 in wages, 1 allowance claimed _____

   $270 in wages, 3 allowances claimed _____

   $315 in wages, 0 allowances claimed _____

2. Why might a single person claim more than 1 allowance?

   _____

3. Why might an individual not claim any allowances (put down 0) even though he or she is entitled to allowances?

   _____

   _____

4. Under what circumstances might you claim exemption from withholding?

   _____

   _____

5. A single person making $240 weekly and claiming 1 allowance would have $15 withheld for income taxes. A married person making $240 weekly and claiming 1 allowance would have $5 withheld. Do you think this difference is fair? Why or why not?

   _____

   _____

Date _____

Fill in the correct word(s) in the spaces provided.

1. The state of feeling worried or uneasy: __ __ __ __ __ __ __

2. Program provided in many organizations for new employees:
__ __ __ __ __ __ __ __ __ __ __

3. The form most commonly filled out by new employees: __-__

4. The power or rank to give orders and make assignments to others:
__ __ __ __ __ __ __ __ __

5. The duty to follow an order or carry out an assignment:
__ __ __ __ __ __ __ __ __ __ __ __ __

6. Shows the flow of authority and responsibility in a company:
__ __ __ __ __ __ __ __ __ __ __   __ __ __ __ __

7. Assigns a task or responsibility to others: __ __ __ __ __ __ __ __ __

8. Entry-level employees usually have a lot of __ __ __ __ __ __ __ __ __ __ __ __ __ __ __ __
and little or no __ __ __ __ __ __ __ __ __.

9. Answering to a supervisor: __ __ __ __ __ __ __ __ __ __ __   __ __   __ __ __ __ __ __ __ __ __ __

10. This is based on rank or the chain of command: __ __ __ __ __ __
__ __ __ __ __ __ __ __

11. This usually involves working for a specific person for a short time or for a certain assignment:
__ __ __ __ __ __ __ __   __ __ __ __ __ __ __ __ __

12. A mood or spirit, such as the attitude and emotion of employees: __ __ __ __ __ __ __

13. A booklet that explains company policies and rules: __ __ __ __ __ __   __ __ __ __ __ __ __

14. One place where you might find policies and rules: __ __ __ __ __ __ __ __
__ __ __ __ __

15. To pay back money already spent: __ __ __ __ __ __ __ __ __

16. The legal right to be notified of a complaint against you and to state your case or
point of view before a decision is made: __ __ __   __ __ __ __ __ __ __ __

17. A trial period during which one's performance is observed and evaluated:
__ __ __ __ __ __ __ __ __

18. Boss: __ __ __ __ __ __ __ __ __

19. Something you should ask your boss for: __ __ __ __ __ __ __ __ __

20. Something you should not ask your boss for: __ __ __ __ __ __ __
__ __ __ __ __ __ __ __

21. Tax exemptions you are entitled to claim: __ __ __ __ __ __ __ __ __ __

22. Not required to pay taxes: __ __ __ __ __ __

CHAPTER 7 Expectations of Employers

7.1 **Expectations of Employers**
Objective: To identify the term or concept associated with various employer expectations regarding job performance, work habits, and attitudes

7.2 **Cost of Lost Production**
Objective: To recognize the extent of financial losses incurred by employers when workers waste time on the job

7.3 **Rating Work Behavior**
Objective: To rate and analyze your performance on the job

Name _____

Date _____

Complete the following crossword puzzle by identifying the correct terms having to do with job performance, work habits, and attitudes.

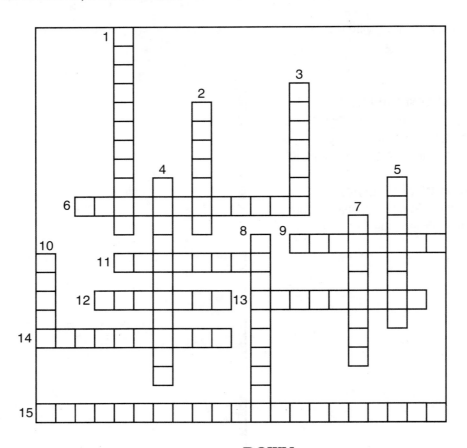

ACROSS

6. Worker output

9. Showing adult behavior

11. A feeling of excitement and involvement

12. Believing in and being devoted to something

13. Tools and machines

14. Eagerness or a strong interest in something

15. The process of judging how well an employee is doing on the job (2 words)

DOWN

1. Getting along with others

2. Not stealing or cheating

3. _____ of work; how well a job is performed

4. Being on time

5. Result of lack of safety consciousness

7. Thinking about a problem and making the right decision

8. Being at work when you are supposed to

10. A feeling of satisfaction with what you or someone you know has accomplished or possesses

When you are late to work, leave early, or "goof off," it costs the company money. Suppose that you earn $6.50 an hour and work 250 days a year. You waste 10 minutes a day. The cost of lost production (CLP) can be computed by the following formula. The production cost is figured at 2 times the hourly rate. It may be more or less depending on the actual company involved.

$$\text{CLP} = \text{production cost} \times \text{hours lost} \times \text{days worked}$$

$$\text{CLP} = \$13.00 \times \frac{10}{60} \times 250$$

$$\text{CLP} = \$13.00 \times .17 \times 250$$

$$\text{CLP} = \$552.50$$

Problem: Assume that Richard earns $7.60 an hour and works 250 days a year. He is 5 minutes late to work, leaves 5 minutes early, and takes 5 extra minutes at lunch. Answer these questions.

1. How much does Richard cost the company each year in lost production? _____

2. Richard is not alone; there are 20 more employees in the company just like him. How much do all of them cost the company per year?

_____

3. Richard is 30 minutes late one morning. He works in a group with 5 other workers who earn the same wage as he does. The group cannot do anything until he arrives. How much does it cost the company to have 6 people waste 30 minutes of production time?

_____

4. Richard was looking forward to a fat year-end bonus. However, the boss said that production was down during the year and there would be no bonuses. Richard and his buddies feel that the company cheated them out of their bonuses. What is your opinion?

_____

_____

_____

_____

5. Many companies dock employees for being late. Do you think this is fair? Why or why not?

_____

_____

_____

_____

Name _____

Date _____

How well are you doing in your job? Rate yourself on these ten items having to do with job performance, work habits, and attitudes. Circle the number that corresponds to your rating in each area. If you do not have a job, rate your behavior in terms of your schoolwork.

	Excellent	Very Good	Average	Fair	Poor
1. Productivity	5	4	3	2	1
2. Quality of work	5	4	3	2	1
3. Judgment	5	4	3	2	1
4. Safety consciousness	5	4	3	2	1
5. Care of equipment	5	4	3	2	1
6. Attendance and punctuality	5	4	3	2	1
7. Cooperation	5	4	3	2	1
8. Interest and enthusiasm	5	4	3	2	1
9. Honesty	5	4	3	2	1
10. Loyalty	5	4	3	2	1

After you have rated yourself, show your ratings to your job supervisor or teacher. Are there areas in which you have rated yourself too low?

_____

_____

Are there areas in which you have rated yourself too high?

_____

_____

What are your weakest areas? What can you do to improve in these areas?

_____

_____

_____

_____

_____

CHAPTER 8 Worker Rights and Protections

8.1 **Worker Rights and Protections**
Objective: To summarize the requirements regarding fair employment practices for the state in which you live

8.2 **Equal Employment Opportunity**
Objective: To name the term or concept associated with various equal opportunity principles and practices

8.3 **Labor-Management Relations**
Objective: To recognize the position of each party on a representative labor-management issue

Use what you have learned in this chapter about worker rights and protections to answer the following questions. You will need to research state and federal laws for some questions.

1. Jaime works at a large aircraft engine plant. He and his wife are planning to adopt a six-year-old girl. Jaime would like to have some time off to be with his new daughter. Is Jaime entitled to leave under state or federal law? Write down the name of the law with the higher standard (state or federal), how much leave Jaime is entitled to, and any conditions (such as whether the leave is paid or unpaid).

_____

_____

_____

2. Milly is one of five female machine operators at a factory. She and the other women have learned that they are being paid substantially less than male factory operators who perform the same kind of work. The factory is not a union shop. Milly has followed her company's procedures for addressing the problem without success. What should she do next?

_____

_____

_____

_____

3. Wendy is a new employee at an auto collision repair shop. Today she is given a new kind of solvent to use to clean car parts before painting. Wendy reads the directions and sees that hazardous fumes can be created if the solvent is not properly prepared. She points this out to the more experienced coworker she's been assigned to work with. He tells her not to worry about it and starts to mix the solvent the way it's always been done. What should Wendy do?

_____

_____

4. Josefina is a work experience student working at a restaurant as a chef's assistant. She has noticed that one of the cooks frequently fails to wash her hands between food preparation steps, which include handling raw meat. What should Josefina do?

_____

_____

Complete the following word puzzle by filling in the correct terms.

1					D						
2					I						
3					S						
4					C						
5					R						
6					I						
7					M						
8					I						
9					N						
10					A						
11					T						
12					I						
13					O						
14					N						

1. Level of government that has acted to protect equal employment opportunity

2. Action that is designed to remedy past discrimination

3. Laws that have been passed, such as those to protect equal employment opportunity

4. Something that equal employment opportunity legislation provides

5. Groups that have been discriminated against

6. Equal treatment

7. Group that has been discriminated against because of its sex

8. _____ and Medical Leave Act

9. The legislative body that passes federal laws

10. Individuals who served in the Armed Forces and who are covered by affirmative action

11. Something provided by equal employment practices

12. Group for whom equal employment opportunity was extended in 1973

13. Federal agency that enforces equal employment opportunity legislation

14. Former President of the United States who first promoted affirmative action

Investigate a recent strike or other labor-management disagreement in your community or state. Identify the main issue and explain the position of each party.

Issue: _____ _____ _____

_____

_____

Labor Position   ←———————→   Management Position

_____	_____
_____	_____
_____	_____
_____	_____
_____	_____
_____	_____
_____	_____
_____	_____
_____	_____

Describe how the issue was finally resolved and what the terms of the settlement were.

_____

_____

_____

Did either party win, or was the outcome a compromise? Explain. _____

_____

_____

_____

_____

_____

CHAPTER 9 Human Relations at Work

9.1 Interpersonal Relations
Objective: To analyze an interpersonal relations problem that you have had with a family member, employer (or teacher), and coworker (or fellow student)

9.2 Customer Relations
Objective: To describe an appropriate response to various types of customer relations situations

9.3 Working in Groups
Objectives: To analyze good and bad experiences working in groups, to list suggestions for working effectively in groups, and to research the topic of working in groups

9.4 Special Human Relations Skills
Objective: To provide examples of occupational situations requiring special human relations skills

Name _____

Date _____

Identify and describe an interpersonal relations problem that you have had with the following individuals. Then explain how the problem might have been avoided by different behavior on your part.

With a family member

1. Problem: _____

_____

_____

2. How avoided: _____

_____

_____

_____

With an employer (or teacher)

3. Problem: _____

_____

_____

4. How avoided: _____

_____

_____

_____

With a coworker (or fellow student)

5. Problem: _____

_____

_____

6. How avoided: _____

_____

_____

_____

Name _____

Date _____

Assume that you are working in a retail store. Explain how you should or might respond to each of these situations.

1. A customer you have never seen before comes into the store _____

   _____

   _____

   _____

2. A frequent, well-known customer comes into the store _____

   _____

   _____

   _____

3. A customer just wants to look around _____

   _____

   _____

   _____

4. A customer returns a product after getting home and deciding that he does not like it

   _____

   _____

   _____

5. A customer returns a defective product and is irate because it does not work _____

   _____

   _____

   _____

6. A customer seems intent on wanting to buy an article of clothing that does not fit right or

   look good on her _____

   _____

   _____

   _____

(Continued on next page)

7. A customer claims you have charged him too much for a purchase _____

_____

_____

_____

8. A customer asks you to suggest a gift item for someone "just your size" _____

_____

_____

_____

9. You observe a customer stealing something _____

_____

_____

_____

10. A customer is about to leave the store without having bought anything _____

_____

_____

_____

11. A customer is preparing to pay for an item that is priced $10 too low _____

_____

_____

_____

12. A customer is about to buy a $200 item that is going to be marked down 30 percent

tomorrow _____

_____

_____

_____

Name _____

Date _____

1. List two good experiences that you have had working in groups. Explain why they were good experiences. _____

   _____

   _____

   _____

   _____

2. List two bad experiences that you have had working in groups. Explain why they were bad experiences. _____

   _____

   _____

   _____

   _____

3. Pages 125–126 of the text give guidelines for working effectively in a group. List two additional suggestions. _____

   _____

   _____

4. In a magazine or newspaper or on the Internet, find an article on working in groups. Print or copy the article, read it, highlight important points, and summarize it.

   _____

   _____

   _____

   _____

   _____

   _____

   _____

   _____

Name _____

Date _____

Some occupations require special human relations skills beyond those explained in Chapter 9. They may involve dealing with circumstances such as accident or illness, danger, death, uncooperative behavior, unwelcome or distressing news, and violence. For each occupation below, provide an example of a situation requiring special human relations skills.

Attorney: _____

_____

Dentist: _____

_____

Flight attendant: _____

_____

High school principal: _____

_____

Hotel counter clerk: _____

_____

Insurance agent: _____

_____

911 dispatcher: _____

_____

Physical therapist: _____

_____

Police officer: _____

_____

Public relations specialist: _____

_____

Undertaker: _____

_____

Veterinarian: _____

_____

CHAPTER 10 Earnings and Job Advancement

10.1 **Your Paycheck**
Objective: To figure earnings and deductions for a sample paycheck

10.2 **Figuring Compensation**
Objective: To calculate various types of compensation

10.3 **Letter of Resignation**
Objective: To write a sample letter of resignation

Refer to the sample pay statement and answer the following questions as if you are the payee.

EMPLOYEE'S PAY STATEMENT
DETACH AND RETAIN FOR YOUR RECORDS

HOURS	EARNINGS			FEDERAL INC TAX	FICA	STATE INC TAX	INSURANCE	NET PAY
	REG	OVERTIME	TOTAL					
45	280.00	52.50	332.50	28.00	25.44	8.00	8.75	262.31

PEN-MART, INC.   **PAYROLL CHECK**   **01462**

January 10, 20 _-- ____

PAY TO THE ORDER OF ____ **Jill Yount** _____ $ **262.31** ____

____ Two hundred sixty-two and $\frac{31}{100}$ _____ DOLLARS

First City Bank
MIDDLETON, VERMONT

Jay Whitney
TREASURER

1. How many hours did you work this pay period? _____

2. What was your regular pay? Overtime pay? _____ _____

3. What was the amount of your gross earnings? _____

4. How much was withheld for federal income tax? State income tax? _____

_____

5. How much was deducted for Social Security tax? _____

6. What was the amount withheld for insurance? _____

7. What were the total deductions for this pay period? _____

8. What percent of your gross pay was withheld? _____

9. If you work the same number of hours for the next three weeks, what will be your total net pay for the month? _____

10. Why is it important to check your pay statement for accuracy and keep it for your records?

_____

_____

Figure the following problems related to work compensation.

1. Pete earns $5.35 an hour for a $37\frac{1}{2}$-hour week. How much does he earn per week?

   _____ Per month? _____

2. Wilma makes $315 per week. She works 50 weeks and gets paid for a 2-week vacation. How

   much is her annual pay? _____

3. Carl receives $6.10 an hour for the first 40 hours he works and time and a half for

   overtime. If he works 45 hours, how much does he earn for the week? _____

4. Evan is paid $590 biweekly. How much does he make per week? _____ Per month?

   _____

5. Michael receives a monthly salary of $2,500 plus a commission of 2% of total orders written.

   If his orders for the month were $34,000, what is his total pay? _____

6. Lisa sold a house for $94,000. The commission is 6%. She gets 3% and the buyer's broker

   gets 3%. How much commission did Lisa earn on the sale? _____

7. Kim works from 6 to 11 on Friday and Saturday evenings at Lombardi's Italian Restaurant.

   She gets $5.75 an hour plus tips. Her tips were $27.35 on Friday and $32.10 on Saturday.

   How much did she earn for the 2 nights' work? _____ How much did she average

   per hour? _____

8. Roger is a teacher who earns $36,000 for the 9-month school year. However, his salary is

   paid out in 12 monthly installments. How much does he get per month? _____

9. Doug packs boxes at the rate of $.55 per box. He averages 12 boxes per hour. How much

   does he earn in an 8-hour day? _____

10. Brenda earned $26,000 last year and received a 15% year-end bonus. What were her total

    earnings? _____

Assume that you have been employed as a work experience education student/learner at Solar Tech, Inc., 4 Main St., Yuma, AZ 85364-1218. At the end of the school year, you are going to enter the Army. Write an appropriate letter of resignation to your supervisor, Ms. Kim Lee.

_____

_____

_____

_____

_____

_____

_____

Dear _____

_____

_____

_____

_____

_____

_____

_____

_____

_____

_____

_____

_____

Sincerely

_____

CHAPTER 11 Appearance on the Job

11.1 Personal Hygiene
Objective: To name terms and concepts associated with personal hygiene

11.2 Hairstyling and Hair Care
Objective: To recognize that choice of a hairstyle may be based on one's facial features and hair characteristics

11.3 Dressing for the Job
Objective: To recognize that jobs have different dress requirements

Name _____

Date _____

A good appearance on the job begins with personal hygiene. Test how much you know about hygiene by matching the phrase in the right-hand column with the correct term on the left. Not all answers are in the textbook.

_____	1. Personal hygiene	a.	Black-tipped plug clogging a pore
_____	2. Pores	b.	Fluid secreted by sweat glands
_____	3. Deodorant	c.	Care of teeth and gums
_____	4. Perspiration	d.	Germs that cause odor
_____	5. Bacteria	e.	Bad breath
_____	6. Acne	f.	Keeping one's body clean and healthy
_____	7. Hormones	g.	Excess flaking of dead skin on scalp
_____	8. Blackhead	h.	Openings in skin
_____	9. Pimple	i.	Tooth decay
_____	10. Hair follicles	j.	Product used to control underarm perspiration odor
_____	11. Dandruff	k.	Common skin condition
_____	12. Dermatologist	l.	Infected pore
_____	13. Oral hygiene	m.	Small cavities in skin containing growing hair and oil-secreting glands
_____	14. Caries	n.	Body chemicals that regulate or stimulate functions; e.g., that stimulate glands to produce oil
_____	15. Halitosis	o.	Doctor who treats skin problems

What hygiene or personal care considerations are particularly important in the occupation for which you are training or that you hope to follow?

_____

_____

_____

_____

_____

Name _____

Date _____

You should choose a hairstyle that goes well with your facial features and hair characteristics. Place a check in the space corresponding to your primary facial shape. Also check all of the hair characteristics that apply to you.

Facial Shape   **Hair Characteristics**

_____ Oval   _____ Thick

                                                  _____ Fine or limp

                                                  _____ Coarse

_____ Long   _____ Curly

                                                  _____ Dry

                                                  _____ Oily

_____ Round   _____ Split or dry ends

                                                  _____ Dandruff

_____ Square

_____ Heart-shaped

Based on your facial shape, what would be a good hairstyle for you?

_____

_____

_____

Based on your characteristics, what type of care does your hair require?

_____

_____

_____

Name _____

Date _____

Dressing appropriately for a job may involve more than simply looking good. Rate the following factors in terms of how important they are in your job (or a job of interest).

Type of job: _____

	Very Important	**Important**	**Of Little Importance**	**Not Important**
Appearance	_____	_____	_____	_____
Comfort	_____	_____	_____	_____
Protection	_____	_____	_____	_____
Sanitation	_____	_____	_____	_____
Durability	_____	_____	_____	_____

Describe the attire of a worker in the above type of job who would be considered appropriately dressed.

_____

_____

_____

_____

Give examples of types of jobs in which each of the following dress factors are of prime importance.

Appearance: _____

_____

Comfort: _____

_____

Protection: _____

_____

Sanitation: _____

_____

Durability: _____

_____

CHAPTER 12 Career Decision Making

12.1 The Decision-making Process
Objective: To use the decision-making process to make and implement a decision

12.2 Decision-making Styles
Objective: To recognize the characteristic approach used in various styles of decision making

12.3 Influences on Decision Making
Objective: To describe and illustrate how various factors influence decision making

Name _____

Date _____

Assume that you and several of your friends plan to go to a movie this weekend. Use the five-step decision-making process to decide which movie to go to (including the theater and time) and implement the decision. Summarize what you did at each step. Then evaluate the results. Even though choosing a movie is not a major decision, it will provide a good illustration of the process.

1. Defining the problem: _____

_____

_____

2. Gathering information: _____

_____

_____

_____

_____

3. Evaluating the information: _____

_____

_____

_____

_____

4. Making a choice: _____

_____

_____

5. Taking action: _____

_____

_____

6. How did the exercise turn out? Did you make a good decision? _____

_____

_____

_____

Name _____

Date _____

Assume that high school graduation is coming up shortly. What are you going to do after graduation? Explain how someone who uses the following decision-making styles would approach this decision. Then identify your decision-making style.

1. The agonizer: _____

_____

_____

2. The mystic: _____

_____

_____

3. The fatalist: _____

_____

_____

4. The evader: _____

_____

_____

5. The plunger: _____

_____

_____

6. The submissive: _____

_____

_____

7. The planner: _____

_____

_____

8. Which decision-making style do you use? _____

_____

Name _____

Date _____

1. Describe a decision that you have made that was influenced by a *previous decision.*

   _____

   _____

   _____

2. Describe a decision that you have made that was influenced by *environment.*

   _____

   _____

   _____

3. Describe a decision that you have made that was influenced by *experience.*

   _____

   _____

   _____

4. Describe a decision that you have made that was influenced by *real-world restrictions.*

   _____

   _____

   _____

5. List several *reality factors* that influence educational and occupational decisions.

   _____

   _____

   _____

6. Give an illustration of someone (acquaintance, family member, famous person) who has

   overcome a reality factor to achieve a goal or to become successful. _____

   _____

   _____

   _____

CHAPTER 13 Information About Your Self

13.1 **Learning About Your Self**
Objective: To explain the meaning and implications of self-information concepts

13.2 **Surveying Employees**
Objective: To survey employed adults about job satisfaction, interests, aptitudes, and work values

13.3 **Rating Interests**
Objective: To identify your interests and relate them to occupations

13.4 **Rating Aptitudes**
Objective: To identify your aptitudes and relate them to occupations

13.5 **Rating Work Values**
Objective: To identify your work values and relate them to occupations

Name _____

Date _____

1. Explain what is meant by the following sentence from your text: "Before you select an occupation, you should first answer the question, 'Who am I?'"

    _____

    _____

2. Explain how the following types of self-information can assist you in making occupational decisions.

    Interests: _____

    _____

    _____

    Aptitudes: _____

    _____

    _____

    Work values: _____

    _____

    _____

    _____

3. When your work experience job ends, will you seek a job in the same occupation? Explain your answer in relation to what you have learned about your self.

    _____

    _____

    _____

4. A job is only a part of life. Describe what you can do in your life to express interests, aptitudes, and work values not being met on the job.

    _____

    _____

    _____

    _____

Name _____

Date _____

Interview two employed adults. Ask them the following questions. Record the answers below.

1. How satisfied are you with your job?

	Completely Satisfied	Somewhat Satisfied	Somewhat Dissatisfied	Completely Dissatisfied
Adult 1				
Adult 2				

2. What are the two most satisfying things about your job?

Adult 1   1. _____

             2. _____

Adult 2   1. _____

             2. _____

3. What are the two least satisfying things about your job?

Adult 1   1. _____

             2. _____

Adult 2   1. _____

             2. _____

4. Do you have interests, aptitudes, and work values that are not met in your job?

	Yes	No
Adult 1		
Adult 2		

5. If you answered yes, what are these interests, aptitudes, and work values, and what do you do in your life to express them?

Adult 1   _____

             _____

             _____

Adult 2   _____

             _____

             _____

Name _____

Date _____

Listed below and on the next four pages are a number of work activities found in a broad range of industries and occupations. Show whether you would like doing each activity by circling one of the three choices as follows:

L = I would like this activity.
? = I am not certain whether I would like or dislike it.
D = I would not like this activity.

You may circle the **L** even if you do not have training for or experience in an activity. Circle the **?** only when you cannot decide whether you would like or dislike an activity or when you do not know what the activity is.

GROUP 1

Prepare and verify financial reports	L	?	D
Develop a budget for an organization	L	?	D
Administer health and safety regulations	L	?	D
Help job seekers find employment	L	?	D
Forecast needs and costs for a research project	L	?	D
Direct department activities for a large company	L	?	D
Manage a hospital or clinic	L	?	D
Develop a detailed marketing strategy	L	?	D
Purchase goods and services for an organization	L	?	D
Analyze information in an insurance application	L	?	D

GROUP 2

Design houses and other buildings	L	?	D
Measure and map land surfaces	L	?	D
Study plants and animals and their environments	L	?	D
Develop new drugs and other chemical compounds	L	?	D
Use math to solve engineering problems	L	?	D
Design and develop tools and machines	L	?	D
Study the earth's atmosphere	L	?	D
Operate television broadcast equipment	L	?	D
Write computer software	L	?	D
Assist engineers and scientists in research	L	?	D

(Continued on next page)

Name _____

Date _____

GROUP 3

Counsel people with problems	L	?	D
Conduct religious services	L	?	D
Defend a client in a criminal trial	L	?	D
Conduct research on human behavior	L	?	D
Plan and direct recreational activities	L	?	D
Teach in a school or college	L	?	D
Help users locate library materials	L	?	D
Administer and interpret personality tests	L	?	D
Maintain a collection of historical documents	L	?	D
Conduct research and write articles and books	L	?	D

GROUP 4

Cut and style hair	L	?	D
Prepare and cook restaurant meals	L	?	D
Guard prisoners in a correctional facility	L	?	D
Fight fires in homes and buildings	L	?	D
Serve passengers on an airplane	L	?	D
Provide security at a bank	L	?	D
Serve food and drinks in a hotel	L	?	D
Investigate a burglary	L	?	D
Provide care for preschool children	L	?	D
Provide janitorial services	L	?	D

GROUP 5

Diagnose and treat vision problems	L	?	D
Provide medical exams and treat ill patients	L	?	D
Care for pets and sick animals	L	?	D
Provide hospital nursing care	L	?	D
Dispense prescription drugs	L	?	D
Provide physical therapy to an accident victim	L	?	D
Administer speech and hearing tests	L	?	D
Conduct medical laboratory tests	L	?	D
Assist surgeons in an operating room	L	?	D
Take medical x-rays	L	?	D

GROUP 6

Write articles and short stories	L	?	D
Edit work of other writers	L	?	D
Design fabrics or fashions	L	?	D
Paint or sketch pictures	L	?	D
Photograph people, places, and events	L	?	D
Direct plays	L	?	D
Play a musical instrument	L	?	D
Sing as a performing artist	L	?	D
Perform a dance routine	L	?	D
Plan publicity for an organization	L	?	D

(Continued on next page)

Name _____

Date _____

GROUP 7

Perform office and clerical work	L	?	D
Operate a cash register	L	?	D
Make travel reservations	L	?	D
Pay and receive money at a bank	L	?	D
Sell merchandise and services to individuals and businesses	L	?	D
Sort and deliver mail	L	?	D
Keep records and perform bookkeeping	L	?	D
Operate computers and business machines	L	?	D
Assist customers in a department store	L	?	D
Greet customers and provide information	L	?	D

GROUP 8

Inspect and repair aircraft engines	L	?	D
Repair and paint auto bodies	L	?	D
Service and repair autos and trucks	L	?	D
Repair and maintain electronic equipment and appliances	L	?	D
Install telephones and communications equipment	L	?	D
Install and repair industrial machinery	L	?	D
Drive trucks or buses	L	?	D
Operate construction and other heavy equipment	L	?	D
Operate and maintain ships and boats	L	?	D
Operate trains, subways, and streetcars	L	?	D

GROUP 9

Lay stones and bricks	L	?	D
Build houses and other small buildings	L	?	D
Install and finish drywall and plaster	L	?	D
Build forms and pour and finish concrete	L	?	D
Install electrical wiring	L	?	D
Paint and paper walls	L	?	D
Install and repair plumbing and fixtures	L	?	D
Fabricate and install sheet metal objects	L	?	D
Construct bridges, towers, and structural metal framework	L	?	D
Install ceramic and other building tiles	L	?	D

GROUP 10

Sew and assemble clothing and other goods	L	?	D
Assemble manufactured products in a factory	L	?	D
Butcher meat, poultry, and fish	L	?	D
Operate electric power-generating equipment	L	?	D
Set up and operate machine tools	L	?	D
Grind and finish eyeglass lenses	L	?	D
Inspect and grade manufactured products	L	?	D
Operate woodworking machines	L	?	D
Develop and print photographs	L	?	D
Cut and weld metals	L	?	D

(Continued on next page)

GROUP 11

Raise crops and livestock	L ? D
Manage a farm for another owner	L ? D
Grow fruits, vegetables, and flowers	L ? D
Trap lobsters, crabs, and other shellfish	L ? D
Net and hook fish and marine life	L ? D
Plant tree seedlings	L ? D
Operate a fishing vessel	L ? D
Harvest trees for lumber and pulp	L ? D
Inspect and grade lumber	L ? D
Oversee maintenance of farm equipment	L ? D

GROUP 12

Capture or destroy enemy ground forces	L ? D
Lead combat soldiers into battle	L ? D
Operate tanks and armored vehicles	L ? D
Fly combat aircraft	L ? D
Direct crews that launch ballistic missiles	L ? D
Fire artillery guns and large shells	L ? D
Construct bunkers and gun emplacements	L ? D
Gather military intelligence	L ? D
Perform search and rescue operations	L ? D
Parachute into battle	L ? D

Interpret your ratings by adding up the number of **L**'s that are circled within each group. Place the totals in the spaces to the right of the group descriptions.

Group Descriptions	Total
1. MANAGERIAL: Interest in directing operations and controlling major activities of an organization	_____
2. SCIENCE AND TECHNOLOGY: Interest in discovering information about the natural world and in using mathematics, science, and technology to solve problems	_____
3. HUMAN SERVICES: Interest in collecting, analyzing, and communicating information and in helping others with their personal, social, and spiritual needs	_____
4. PERSONAL AND PUBLIC SERVICES: Interest in providing services for the convenience of others and in using authority to protect people and property	_____
5. HEALTH SERVICES: Interest in diagnosing and treating illnesses, accidents, and diseases and providing direct patient care and supportive clinical services	_____

(Continued on next page)

Name _____

Date _____

Group Descriptions   **Total**

6. ARTS AND COMMUNICATIONS: Interest in creative   _____
   expression of ideas or feelings

7. BUSINESS AND MARKETING: Interest in organized, clearly   _____
   defined office activities and in selling products and services

8. MECHANICAL: Interest in installing, servicing, and repairing   _____
   equipment and machines and in operating transportation
   equipment

9. CONSTRUCTION: Interest in using hand tools and power   _____
   equipment to construct homes, buildings, and other structures

10. PRODUCTION: Interest in concrete, repetitive, organized   _____
    activities, primarily in a factory setting

11. NATURAL RESOURCES: Interest in activities involving   _____
    plants and animals, primarily in an outdoor setting

12. MILITARY: Interest in possible military combat as a member   _____
    of the Armed Forces

For which group do you have the highest total? _____

Now, turn to Part 2 of this workbook and read about the nature of work performed within your preferred group. Read the occupational descriptions and list below the five in which you are most interested.

_____   _____   _____

_____   _____

Aptitudes are natural talents or developed abilities. For each aptitude listed, rate yourself in terms of whether you have a *low, average,* or *high* degree of that aptitude. Circle the appropriate number.

VERBAL	**Low**		**Average**		**High**
■ Ability to express yourself in writing	1	2	3	4	5
■ Ability to talk before a group	1	2	3	4	5
■ Ability to understand the meaning of words	1	2	3	4	5
■ Ability to understand what you have read	1	2	3	4	5

NUMERICAL

■ Ability to perform math quickly and accurately	1	2	3	4	5
■ Ability to solve math story problems	1	2	3	4	5
■ Ability to analyze and interpret a large amount of data	1	2	3	4	5
■ Ability to work with math formulas and symbols	1	2	3	4	5

CLERICAL

■ Ability to find important information in written materials and tables	1	2	3	4	5
■ Ability to see differences in written materials	1	2	3	4	5
■ Ability to proofread words and numbers	1	2	3	4	5
■ Ability to record numerical data correctly	1	2	3	4	5

MANUAL DEXTERITY

■ Ability to coordinate eyes and hands quickly and accurately	1	2	3	4	5
■ Ability to react quickly	1	2	3	4	5
■ Ability to manipulate small objects with the fingers	1	2	3	4	5
■ Ability to work with the hands in placing and turning motions	1	2	3	4	5

(Continued on next page)

Name _____

Date _____

MECHANICAL REASONING	Low		Average		High
■ Ability to understand how tools and machines operate	1	2	3	4	5
■ Ability to understand how wheels, gears, and pulleys transform motion and energy	1	2	3	4	5
■ Ability to understand the practical meaning of differences in weight, size, shape, volume, and balance	1	2	3	4	5
■ Ability to select the more efficient of two different methods of performing work	1	2	3	4	5

SPATIAL VISUALIZATION					
■ Ability to visualize geometric forms in your mind	1	2	3	4	5
■ Ability to visualize what a three-dimensional object looks like in two dimensions	1	2	3	4	5
■ Ability to visually recognize changes resulting from changing the position of a three-dimensional object	1	2	3	4	5
■ Ability to visualize hidden surfaces of a three-dimensional object	1	2	3	4	5

Interpret your ratings. For which two types of aptitudes do you have the highest ratings?

_____   _____

Name five different occupations for which your two highest aptitudes would be important.

_____   _____

_____   _____

_____

Turn to Part 2 of this workbook and read the descriptions for the above occupations. Do the occupations relate to your highest-rated aptitudes? Explain.

_____

_____

_____

_____

Name _____

Date _____

Read each statement and decide how important it is in choosing the type of work you would like to do. Rate the statements as follows:

3 = Very important
2 = Important
1 = Unimportant

1. Planning your own activities _____

2. Not getting laid off _____

3. Helping other people _____

4. Doing a job well _____

5. Having a good place to work _____

6. Doing a variety of things _____

7. Creating something new _____

8. Having others look up to you _____

9. Being around nice people _____

10. Getting big raises _____

11. Making a contribution to society _____

12. Being your own boss _____

13. Doing different things _____

14. Earning an above-average income _____

15. Knowing your job is permanent _____

16. Trying out a new idea _____

17. Admiring something you have done _____

18. Having pleasant surroundings _____

19. Doing a good deed _____

20. Earning enough to live well _____

21. Creating a better way of doing something _____

22. Deciding things yourself _____

23. Seeing your name in print _____

24. Being able to count on having a job _____

25. Having a varied schedule _____

26. Feeling good about your work _____

27. Being recognized in your field _____

Referring to the chart on the next page, interpret your ratings by adding the numbers together for each type of work value. As an example, for altruism, add together your ratings for Items 3, 11, and 19. Place the number in the chart.

(Continued on next page)

Name _____

Date _____

Work Value	Items	Score	Work Value	Items	Score
Altruism	3, 11, 19	_____	Prestige	8, 23, 27	_____
Creativity	7, 16, 21	_____	Earnings	10, 14, 20	_____
Achievement	4, 17, 26	_____	Security	2, 15, 24	_____
Independence	1, 12, 22	_____	Surroundings	5, 9, 18	_____
			Variety	6, 13, 25	_____

What are your three highest-rated work values?

_____ _____ _____

Summarize what your ratings reveal in terms of what is important to you regarding work.

_____

_____

_____

_____

_____

Name five occupations that you believe are related to your highest-rated work values.

_____ _____ _____

_____ _____

Turn to Part 2 of this workbook and read the descriptions for the above occupations. Do the occupations relate to your highest-rated work values? Explain.

_____

_____

_____

_____

_____

CHAPTER 14 Career Information

14.1 Reading Tables and Charts
Objective: To interpret labor market information contained in tables and charts

14.2 Exploring Occupational Groups
Objective: To explore one of the SOC groups contained in the *OOH*

14.3 Using the Occupational Outlook Handbook
Objective: To learn how to use the *OOH* to conduct an occupational search

14.4 Conducting an Occupational Search
Objective: To explore an occupation using the *OOH*

Name _____

Date _____

Understanding labor market information requires the ability to read tables and charts. Look up the figures in your textbook as directed and answer the following questions.

Employment Changes by Industry. Refer to Figure 14–3 (page 189 of your textbook).

1. Of the ten industries, how many are expected to grow through the year 2008? _____

2. Which industry will grow the most? _____

3. How many industries are expected to decline through the year 2008? _____

4. By how much will Manufacturing and Mining decline? _____% _____%

5. By what percent will employment for the following industries change from 1998 to 2008?

   a. Retail trade _____%   b. Government _____%   c. Construction _____%

Fastest-Growing Occupations. Refer to Figure 14–5 (page 192 of your textbook).

6. How many of the 20 fastest-growing occupations are health-related? _____

7. How many are computer-related? _____

8. Between 1998 and 2008, what will be the growth rate for the following occupations?

   a. Medical assistants _____%   b. Respiratory therapists _____%

   c. Database administrators _____%

9. What type of education and training is required for the majority of occupations shown in

   Figure 14–5? _____

Occupations with Largest Numerical Increases. Refer to Figure 14–6 (page 193 of your textbook).

10. Between 1998 and 2008, how many new jobs will be added for the following occupations?

    a. Registered nurses _____ b. Cashiers _____

    c. Secondary school teachers _____

11. Four occupations in Figure 14–5 are also included in Figure 14–6. Name them:

    _____   _____

    _____   _____

12. What type of education and training is required for the majority of occupations shown in

    Figure 14–6? _____

Name _____

Date _____

Exploring an occupational group (cluster) can help you to discover occupations that you are not aware of or have not thought much about. Turn to Part 2 of this workbook and review the list of 12 occupational clusters. Select one of the groups to explore. Find information about the group in Part 2 and answer the following questions.

Occupational Group: _____

1. Occupations are classified into the 12 groups on the basis of the type of work performed. What type of work do people in this group perform?

   _____

   _____

   _____

   _____

2. In what types of industries are you most likely to find workers from this occupational group?

   _____

   _____

   _____

3. What types of aptitudes are most needed by people who work in this occupational group? (You may wish to review Activity 13.4.)

   _____

   _____

   _____

4. What opportunities does this occupational group seem to offer in terms of allowing you to satisfy your work values? (You may wish to review your work values in Activity 13.5.)

   _____

   _____

   _____

5. Name from one to five occupations found in this group that you would like to learn more about.

   _____   _____   _____

   _____   _____

Name _____

Date _____

This activity will help you learn how to use the *OOH* effectively to conduct an occupational search. Turn to pages 188–190 of this workbook and answer the following questions.

1. In the online *OOH*, what is the best way to find information on occupation clusters?

   _____

2. In the online *OOH*, what are two ways to find information on specific occupations?

   _____   _____

3. In the online *OOH*, where could you read about forces likely to determine employment opportunities in industries and occupations through the year 2010?

   _____

The box on the right below lists six of the eight sections of an *OOH* occupational description. Match the information in the left column with the section where the information can be found.

_____ 4. What workers do

_____ 5. Typical hours worked

_____ 6. The workplace environment

_____ 7. Individual job duties

_____ 8. Typical earnings

_____ 9. Advancement possibilities

_____ 10. Benefits

_____ 11. The most important sources of training

_____ 12. Emerging specialties

_____ 13. Geographic distribution of jobs

_____ 14. The typical length of training

_____ 15. Desirable skills, aptitudes, and personal characteristics

_____ 16. The influence of technological advancements on the way work is done

_____ 17. Factors that will result in growth or decline in the number of jobs

_____ 18. Physical activities and susceptibility to injury

_____ 19. Key industries where jobs are found

_____ 20. The training preferred by employers

_____ 21. The number of jobs the occupation provided in 2000

_____ 22. Susceptibility to layoffs

_____ 23. The relationship between the number of job seekers and openings

a. Nature of the Work

b. Working Conditions

c. Employment

d. Training, Other Qualifications, and Advancement

e. Job Outlook

f. Earnings

Name _____

Date _____

In four previous activities (13.3, 13.4, 13.5, and 14.2), you used different approaches to identify potential occupational preferences. Go back and review these occupations. Select one and use it to conduct an in-depth search in the *Occupational Outlook Handbook*. Find the occupation in the *OOH* and complete the form on this page and the next. An extra master copy of this form appears on pages 247–248.

OCCUPATIONAL SEARCH FORM

TITLE OF THE OCCUPATION _____

NATURE OF THE WORK

List five major tasks that workers in this occupation perform.

1. _____
   _____

2. _____
   _____

3. _____
   _____

4. _____
   _____

5. _____
   _____

WORKING CONDITIONS

Write down the normal working hours, if they are listed. _____
_____

Describe the typical working conditions. _____
_____
_____

Are there any unpleasant or dangerous aspects to this occupation? _____
_____

EMPLOYMENT

Number of jobs in the occupation _____ Year provided _____

In what types of industries or locations do people in this occupation work?

_____

(Continued on next page)

Name _____

Date _____

TRAINING, OTHER QUALIFICATIONS, AND ADVANCEMENT

What is the preferred or required level of education or training? _____

_____

List any licensure or certification requirements. _____

_____

List any special abilities or qualifications recommended or required. _____

_____

What opportunities are there for advancement? _____

JOB OUTLOOK

Check the statement in each column below that best describes the future outlook for this occupation.

Change in Employment

____ Faster than average growth

____ Average growth

____ Slower than average growth

____ Little change

____ Decline

Opportunities and Competition

____ Very good to excellent opportunities

____ Good opportunities

____ May face competition

____ Keen competition

EARNINGS

Write down the average yearly starting salary, if available. _____

Range of average yearly earnings _____ Year provided _____

RELATED OCCUPATIONS

List the titles of related occupations.

1. _____   5. _____

2. _____   6. _____

3. _____   7. _____

4. _____   8. _____

SOURCES OF ADDITIONAL INFORMATION

List names and addresses of places where further information may be obtained.

_____

_____

_____

_____

_____

_____

Source of information: *Occupational Outlook Handbook* 20__/20__ Edition, pages _____

CHAPTER 15

Communication Skills

15.1 Communication Skills
Objective: To name terms and concepts associated with communication

15.2 Effective Listening
Objective: To provide examples of different barriers to effective listening

15.3 Spelling and Grammar
Objective: To identify and correct various spelling and grammar errors

15.4 Correcting a Business Form
Objective: To analyze a filled-out form and suggest improvements

15.5 Writing a Memo
Objective: To practice writing a memo

Name _____

Date _____

Complete the following crossword puzzle by identifying the correct terms having to do with communication skills and processes.

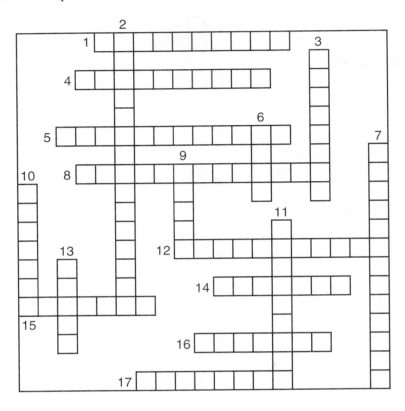

ACROSS

1. The total of all the words you know
4. An example of this is coming to a conclusion before you have heard any or all of the facts.
5. Things that interfere with listening
8. Sending information, ideas, or feelings from one person to another
12. How distinctly or clearly one speaks
14. Written language
15. One way to visually receive information
16. The primary language used in the United States
17. Before sending a message composed on software, you should run the _____ checker.

DOWN

2. An example of this is wanting to challenge what the speaker is saying and then missing the message.
3. Oral communication
6. The most informal type of written business communication
7. The way in which words are spoken
9. A common distraction
10. A set of rules about correct speaking and writing
11. Receiving oral communication and other sounds
13. This is becoming the preferred form of personal and business communication.

Name _____

Date _____

Give an example of each of the following barriers to effective listening. Try to use an example related to a job or school situation.

Distraction: _____

_____

_____

_____

Prejudging: _____

_____

_____

_____

Overstimulation: _____

_____

_____

_____

Partial listening: _____

_____

_____

_____

Have you ever been involved in an accident or other serious situation because of not listening to what you were told? Describe such an incident or give an example that you are familiar with.

_____

_____

_____

_____

_____

_____

■ Activity 15.3 Spelling and Grammar   Name _____

                                             Date _____

Half of the following words are misspelled. Underline the 15 incorrect words. For each incorrect word, write the correctly spelled word on the line to the right.

accesible _____   equipped _____   ninty _____

achievement _____   excillent _____   originel _____

apparant _____   fascinate _____   precede _____

beginner _____   fourty _____   proceed _____

business _____   greevance _____   receipt _____

changable _____   hoping _____   refering _____

committ _____   imediately _____   sense _____

consistent _____   independent _____ transfered _____

decision _____   license _____   usefull _____

desparete _____   medacine _____   weird _____

Circle and then correct the grammatical error in each of the following sentences.

1. I have looked for the wrench, but it ain't here. _____

2. Was you aware of the problem? _____

3. It don't seem like quitting time. _____

4. He might of left the paperwork here. _____

5. I done that same job yesterday. _____

6. She brung the new parts for us to see. _____

7. I seen them unload the new machine. _____

8. This here manual explains how to do it. _____

9. I do not have nothing to lose. _____

10. We could not scarcely see a thing. _____

11. The application of robots are expanding rapidly. _____

12. The pen, pad, and calculator is all here. _____

Jenny works for a roofing company. Yesterday she turned in the following job work order. What would you think of it if you were her supervisor or the customer? List any suggestions you have for Jenny at the bottom of the page. Also, list anything about the form that she did well.

JOB WORK ORDER
No. 4875

CUSTOMER	DATE OF ORDER
Ramona Rivera	5/22/—

STREET ADDRESS
6231 Park

CITY
Chula Vista

TELEPHONE: WORK	HOME
555-0123	

STARTING DATE	DATE COMPLETED
	5/27

DESCRIPTION OF WORK

Front entry roof redone. Replaced the bad wood. Repaint the brick joints on right side chimney & flash lower right side chimney upper right side to. The gutters was cleaned & I painted the roof metal work. Found a lose soffit & renailed it. Replaced some rotted wood on front rake, it was the right side. Fixed hole behind chimney & 10 ft of downspout

PAID BY		MATERIALS	
		LABOR	
❏ Cash			
❏ Credit Card		TAX	
❏ Bill			
❏ Check No. _____		TOTAL	3579.86

SERVICE REP NO.	CUSTOMER'S SIGNATURE
Jenny	*Ramona Rivera*

_____

_____

_____

_____

Assume that you work in the Shipping Department and have discovered several errors on an invoice that is to be sent out along with a carton of goods. Write a memorandum to Terry Foster in the Accounting Department telling him of your discovery and asking him whether to go ahead and ship the goods.

MEMORANDUM

TO: _____

             _____

FROM: _____

             _____

DATE: _____

SUBJECT: _____

_____

_____

_____

_____

_____

_____

_____

_____

_____

_____

_____

_____

_____

_____

CHAPTER 16 Math and Measurement Skills

16.1 **Math and Measurement Terminology**
Objective: To name terms and concepts associated with math and measurement

16.2 **Basic Math**
Objective: To compute the answer to various business math problems

16.3 **Basic Measurement**
Objective: To compute the answer to various measurement problems

■ Activity 16.1 Math and Measurement Terminology

Name _____

Date _____

Fill in the correct word(s) in the spaces provided.

1. Common uses of arithmetic at work: __ __ __ __ __ __ __ __ __ __ __ __

2. The price of one item: __ __ __ __

3. A bill for goods: __ __ __ __ __ __ __

4. A deduction from the catalog (list) price of an item: __ __ __ __ __ __ __ __ __ __ __ __ __ __

5. These state the time limit within which the buyer must pay: __ __ __ __ __ __

6. A reduction in price offered to encourage early payment: __ __ __ __ __ __ __ __ __ __ __ __

7. The price a retailer pays for goods: __ __ __ __

8. An amount added by the retailer to the cost price: __ __ __ __ __ __ __

9. Tax added to the purchase price of goods: __ __ __ __ __

10. A reduction in the selling price of a product: __ __ __ __ __ __ __ __ __

11. The act of determining "how much": __ __ __ __ __ __ __ __ __ __ __

12. The distance around an object: __ __ __ __ __ __ __ __ __

13. The perimeter of a circle: __ __ __ __ __ __ __ __ __ __ __ __ __

14. One-half the diameter of a circle: __ __ __ __ __ __

15. The number of square units of space on the surface of a figure enclosed by the perimeter: __ __ __ __

16. The formula for determining the area of a rectangle: __ __ __ __ __ __ × __ __ __ __ __

17. The constant used in the formula to find the area of a circle: __ . __ __

18. Length, width, and height: __ __ __ __ __ __ __ __ __ __

19. A number that has been multiplied by itself: __ __ __ __ __ __ __

20. The amount of space an object takes up: __ __ __ __ __ __

21. The measure used to express the volume of rectangular objects: __ __ __ __ __ __

22. The process of changing from one unit of measure to another: __ __ __ __ __ __ __ __ __ __ __

23. The most widely used system of measurement: __ __ __ __ __ __

24. The basic unit of measure in the metric system: __ __ __ __ __

25. The basic unit of weight in the metric system: __ __ __ __

Complete the following business math problems. Place your answers in the boxes provided. Use the space at the bottom of each page to make computations if you need it.

Total purchase amount

1.

$8 \times \$ .99 = \$$ _____

$4 \times .35 = \$$ _____

$6 \times 1.43 = \$$ _____

$\$$ [ ]

2.

$7 \times \$ 3.49 = \$$ _____

$12 \times .95 = \$$ _____

$6 \times 12.63 = \$$ _____

$\$$ [ ]

3.

$24 \times \$ 7.50 = \$$ _____

$30 \times 18.90 = \$$ _____

$22 \times 13.27 = \$$ _____

$9 \times 8.07 = \$$ _____

$14 \times 21.65 = \$$ _____

$\$$ [ ]

Trade discount

	4.	**5.**	**6.**	**7.**
List price:	$175.00	$1,470.00	$820.00	$79.00
% discount:	25%	40%	33%	20%
Discount:	$ [ ]	$ [ ]	$ [ ]	$ [ ]
Net purchase price:	$ [ ]	$ [ ]	$ [ ]	$ [ ]

Markup

	8.	**9.**		**10.**	**11.**
Selling price:	$96.00	$250.00	Cost price:	$50.00	$115.00
Cost price:	$60.00	$200.00	% markup:	30%	25%
Markup:	$ [ ]	$ [ ]	Markup:	$ [ ]	$ [ ]
% markup:	[ ] %	[ ] %	Selling price:	$ [ ]	$ [ ]

(Continued on next page)

93

Name _____

Date _____

Sales tax	**12.**	**13.**	**14.**	**15.**
Purchase price:	$48.00	$135.00	$260.00	$94.00
% sales tax:	5%	4%	3.5%	2%
Sales tax:	$ ____	$ ____	$ ____	$ ____
Total amount:	$ ____	$ ____	$ ____	$ ____

Markdown	**16.**	**17.**	**18.**	**19.**
Original price:	$ 60.00	$165.00	$89.50	$324.00
% markdown:	25%	50%	30%	40%
Markdown:	$ ____	$ ____	$ ____	$ ____
Sale price:	$ ____	$ ____	$ ____	$ ____

Name _____

Date _____

Complete the following problems. Carry your answers to two decimal places. Place them in the spaces provided.

Shapes and Dimensions

1. What is the name of each of these common geometric shapes?

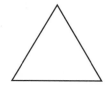   

A. _____   B. _____   C. _____

2. What three main dimensions of a circle are shown below?

A. _____   B. _____   C. _____

Perimeter

3. What is the perimeter of a triangle that is 7.5 feet on each side? _____

4. A carpenter is putting baseboard around a room that is 12 feet long and 10 feet wide. The room has 3 doorways, each 3 feet wide. How many linear feet of molding are needed?

_____

5. Suppose that you must enclose an equipment yard with fencing and have 48 feet of fencing. One side of the rectangular yard will be 6 feet. What will be the dimensions of the equipment yard?

_____

6. What is the circumference in feet of a circle that has a diameter of 3 feet 3 inches?

_____

7. What is the radius of a circle that has a circumference of 12.56 feet? _____

Area

8. What is the area in square feet of a room 22 feet 3 inches long and 12 feet wide?

_____

9. What is the length of a room that contains 252 square feet and is 18 feet wide?

_____

(Continued on next page)

95

10. You need to carpet a room that measures 12 x 21 feet. Carpeting costs $11.95 a square yard. How much will the carpet cost?

_____

11. What is the area in square inches of a circle that has a diameter of 2 feet 4 inches?

_____

12. What is the radius in feet of a circle that contains 78.5 square feet? _____

Volume

13. What is the volume in cubic inches of a rectangular solid that is 6 feet long, 16 inches high, and 3 feet 6 inches wide?

_____

14. A rectangular storage bin measures 18 x 12 x 12 feet. If a struck bushel is equal to 1.24 cubic feet, how many struck bushels of grain would it hold?

_____

15. How many cubic yards of concrete would be required to pour a 6-inch concrete slab that measures 32 x 18 feet?

_____

Metric

16. Express 100 yards in meters. _____

17. If a machine part measures 28 centimeters in length, how long is the part in inches?

_____

18. How many centimeters are there in 3 feet? _____

19. Express 130 pounds in kilograms. _____

20. A crate weighs 20,000 kilograms. How many pounds does it weigh? _____

21. A room that is 12 feet on each side contains how many cubic meters? _____

22. If a truck takes 38 liters to fill, how many gallons does this equal? _____

CHAPTER 17 Safety Skills

17.1 **Preventing Accidents**
Objective: To identify common accidents for a given occupation and how they can be avoided

17.2 **Safety Practices Self-rating**
Objective: To judge yourself in relation to the extent to which you follow various safety practices

17.3 **Auto Safety Check Sheet**
Objective: To conduct a safety inspection of an automobile

17.4 **Safety Organizations**
Objective: To gather and organize information for a short, written report about a safety organization

■ **Activity 17.1 Preventing Accidents**　　　Name _____

　　　　　　　　　　　　　　　　　　　　　　　Date _____

What occupation are you currently preparing for or hoping to follow upon completing your

education or training? _____

Name the five most common accidents involving this occupation. Then, explain how each type
of accident can best be avoided.

1. _____ : _____

　 _____

2. _____ : _____

　 _____

3. _____ : _____

　 _____

4. _____ : _____

　 _____

5. _____ : _____

　 _____

List as many different types of safety devices and equipment as you can think of that are used
in your occupation.

_____

_____

_____

_____

_____

_____

_____

_____

_____

_____

■ Activity 17.2 Safety Practices Self-rating

Name _____

Date _____

Rate yourself on each of the following safety practices.	Always	Usually	Seldom	Never
1. I pick up shoes, books, and other objects from stairs and floors.	_____	_____	_____	_____
2. I put kitchen knives, other utensils, tools, and household cleaners away immediately after use.	_____	_____	_____	_____
3. I use a ladder or firm chair to reach objects in high places.	_____	_____	_____	_____
4. I turn pot handles toward the back of the range.	_____	_____	_____	_____
5. I immediately wipe up water, grease, or anything else spilled on the floor.	_____	_____	_____	_____
6. I dry my hands before using a hair dryer, razor, or other electrical appliance.	_____	_____	_____	_____
7. I keep radios and similar electrical appliances out of the bathroom.	_____	_____	_____	_____
8. I wear a shirt, pants, and heavy work shoes when using a lawn mower.	_____	_____	_____	_____
9. I cooperate with teachers and other school officials in following safety instructions.	_____	_____	_____	_____
10. I do not run, crowd, or shove in school halls or stairways.	_____	_____	_____	_____
11. I do not throw pens, pencils, paper clips, or other objects in school.	_____	_____	_____	_____
12. I learn and obey job safety rules and regulations.	_____	_____	_____	_____
13. I consult the job procedures manual or ask my supervisor or experienced coworkers about things I do not know how to do.	_____	_____	_____	_____
14. I watch for safety hazards on the job.	_____	_____	_____	_____
15. I report job accidents and injuries.	_____	_____	_____	_____
16. I try to set a good example for other workers regarding safety on the job.	_____	_____	_____	_____
17. I perform as trained on the job.	_____	_____	_____	_____
18. I use proper equipment and clothing in recreational activities.	_____	_____	_____	_____

(Continued on next page)

	Always	Usually	Seldom	Never
19. I avoid overexertion in recreation.	_____	_____	_____	_____
20. I do not swim alone or take chances around water.	_____	_____	_____	_____
21. I observe motor vehicle speed limits.	_____	_____	_____	_____
22. I am a courteous driver.	_____	_____	_____	_____
23. I stay a safe distance behind other vehicles when driving.	_____	_____	_____	_____
24. I do not operate motor vehicles under the influence of drugs or alcohol.	_____	_____	_____	_____
25. I use a safety belt when operating a motor vehicle.	_____	_____	_____	_____

How safety-conscious are you? Review the ratings and give yourself an overall safety rating as follows:

_____ Outstanding   _____ Good   _____ Average   _____ Weak

26. In what area of personal accident prevention are you most in need of improvement—home, school, job, recreation, or automobile?

_____

Explain what you need to do to improve in this area.

_____

_____

_____

_____

_____

_____

_____

Name _____

Date _____

Use the following checklist to conduct a safety inspection of your car, the family car, or another vehicle.

Yes No   BRAKES
☐   ☐   Stop car in 25 feet or less from 20 mph

☐   ☐   All four wheels take hold evenly.

☐   ☐   Take hold evenly before brake pedal is 1 inch from floor

☐   ☐   Emergency brake can hold car on any hill.

☐   ☐   Make no scratchy sound when applied

☐   ☐   Brake fluid clean and at proper level

HEADLIGHTS
☐   ☐   Aimed for maximum light on road and minimum glare

☐   ☐   Dimming switch and upper and lower beams in good working order

☐   ☐   Lenses clean and reflectors bright

REAR LIGHTS AND SIGNALS
☐   ☐   Bulbs burn—controls work

☐   ☐   Brakes operate stop light.

☐   ☐   Lenses clean, clear, and free of cracks

☐   ☐   Reflectors in good condition

TIRES
☐   ☐   Treads and sidewalls free from worn spots, cuts, and breaks

☐   ☐   Properly inflated

☐   ☐   Even wear shows wheel alignment OK and no tire rotation necessary

☐   ☐   Ample tread

REARVIEW MIRROR
☐   ☐   Clear, steady view of road behind

☐   ☐   Easily adjusted

(Continued on next page)

Name _____

Date _____

Yes No STEERING AND WHEEL ALIGNMENT
☐ ☐ Play in steering wheel does not exceed $1\frac{1}{2}$ to 3 inches.

☐ ☐ Car steers easily.

EXHAUST SYSTEM AND MUFFLER
☐ ☐ Tight—no carbon monoxide seepage into car through holes or leaks

☐ ☐ Quiet

WINDSHIELD WIPERS
☐ ☐ Dependable—work when needed

☐ ☐ Flexible rubber blades that wipe clean

☐ ☐ Run at an adequate and constant speed

GLASS
☐ ☐ Free from cracks, chips, discoloration, or dirt that obscures vision

☐ ☐ Free from unnecessary stickers and objects that obscure vision

☐ ☐ Clean and free of dirt or film

HORN
☐ ☐ Sounds off when properly depressed

☐ ☐ Loud enough to be heard 200 feet away but not so loud that it is a nuisance

☐ ☐ Operates from any part of horn assembly

OTHER
☐ ☐ Seat belts in good working order

☐ ☐ Flashlight in car

☐ ☐ No objects on back seat that obstruct vision

☐ ☐ Defroster works properly with good flow of air.

☐ ☐ Sun visors work freely, yet stay as positioned.

Adapted from "Unit 1: The Car and the Highway." 4-H Automotive Care and Safety Project.

Name _____

Date _____

Activity 5 on page 251 of your test lists 20 government agencies and private organizations that work in the field of personal and public safety and asks you to research an organization and prepare a short, written report. Use this page and the next to assist you in gathering and organizing the information for your report.

Source

Author(s) _____

Title: _____

_____

Date of publication: _____ Publisher: _____

Place of publication (if on the Web, list the URL): _____

_____ Pages: _____

Notes

When the organization was founded: _____ The purpose of the organization: _____

_____

Types of activities in which it engages: _____

_____

_____

_____

_____

How it is supported: _____

_____

_____

_____

_____

(Continued on next page)

Name _____

Date _____

Other information: _____

_____

_____

_____

_____

_____

_____

Organization

Introduction: _____

_____

Main point and supporting ideas: _____

_____

_____

Main point and supporting ideas: _____

_____

_____

Main point and supporting ideas: _____

_____

_____

Conclusion: _____

_____

_____

CHAPTER 18 Leadership Skills

18.1 **Leadership Characteristics**
Objective: To recall characteristics associated with leadership

18.2 **Career and Technical Student Organizations**
Objective: To describe the purpose, activities, and benefits of membership in a specific career and technical student organization

18.3 **Parliamentary Terms and Procedures**
Objective: To identify terms, concepts, and procedures associated with parliamentary procedure

Circle the letter T for each true statement and the letter F for each false statement.

T   F   1. You can usually tell a leader by his or her appearance.

T   F   2. A leader's message often has to be repeated again and again.

T   F   3. Leaders view information as something to be kept to themselves.

T   F   4. A leader is always the person in charge of a meeting or organization.

T   F   5. Not all leaders are naturally gifted communicators.

T   F   6. Leaders rely primarily on written communications.

T   F   7. Leaders gather and give information through interaction with others.

T   F   8. The best leaders do most of the work themselves.

T   F   9. Leaders provide positive feedback.

T   F   10. A leader helps create a strong team spirit.

T   F   11. Leaders help other people to achieve.

T   F   12. Leaders hold group meetings only when absolutely necessary.

T   F   13. Leaders do not tolerate any mistakes.

T   F   14. Leaders challenge people to stretch and grow.

T   F   15. Most leaders are willing to accept an average level of performance.

T   F   16. The leader's style pulls rather than pushes people on.

T   F   17. Most leaders are not concerned about being a good role model.

T   F   18. A leader's words are much more important than her or his actions.

T   F   19. If a leader slows down, the group will usually speed up to impress the leader.

T   F   20. Leaders often ask tough questions.

T   F   21. A leader is good at solving difficult problems.

T   F   22. Most leaders stick to their work rather than getting involved in community activities.

T   F   23. Leaders know how to focus attention on an issue or problem.

T   F   24. Leaders are often in contact with other businesses and other leaders.

T   F   25. Leadership skills are something a person either is born with or is not.

In Activity 2 on page 266 of your text, you found out the types of career and technical student organizations in your school. In which organization are you most interested? Write the name below and answer the following questions about the organization.

1. What is the purpose of the organization? _____

   _____

   _____

   _____

2. What are five activities conducted by the organization to promote leadership skills and good

   citizenship? _____

   _____

   _____

   _____

   _____

3. What support and opportunities are provided by the national organization? _____

   _____

   _____

   _____

4. How might you personally benefit by joining this organization? _____

   _____

   _____

   _____

   _____

Match the phrase in the right-hand column with the correct term on the left.

_____ 1. Parliamentary procedure   a. The standard steps covered in a meeting

_____ 2. Bylaws   b. A written record of a meeting

_____ 3. Majority   c. These define the basic characteristics of an organization and describe how it will operate.

_____ 4. Quorum   d. Rank of priority

_____ 5. Order of business   e. Rules to conduct a meeting in a fair and orderly manner

_____ 6. Motion   f. A majority of the membership

_____ 7. Precedence   g. An authority on rules

_____ 8. Parliamentarian   h. Support (a motion)

_____ 9. Minutes   i. A brief statement of a proposed action

_____ 10. Second   j. One more than half of the voters

The steps involved in making, discussing, and disposing of a motion are listed below in scrambled order. Number the steps from 1 to 10 in their correct order.

_____ 1. Motion is discussed (debated).

_____ 2. Motion is stated.

_____ 3. Members vote on the motion.

_____ 4. Member obtains the floor by rising and addressing the chair.

_____ 5. Member moves for adjournment.

_____ 6. Chair recognizes the member.

_____ 7. Chair announces results of the vote.

_____ 8. Motion is seconded (usually).

_____ 9. Discussion ends after all who wish to have spoken.

_____ 10. Chair restates the motion.

CHAPTER 19 Computer and Technology Skills

19.1 **Computer Literacy**
Objective: To name terms and concepts associated with computer operation

19.2 **Occupations and Computers**
Objective: To describe how computers are used in relation to an occupation of interest

19.3 **Robots**
Objective: To investigate and prepare a short, written report on robots

19.4 **Working with Spreadsheets, I**
Objective: To create a payroll spreadsheet

19.5 **Working with Spreadsheets, II**
Objective: To explain numerical data with a spreadsheet, chart, and text

Name _____

Date _____

Match the phrase in the right-hand column with the correct term on the left.

_____ 1. Computer   a. Devices located outside the CPU

_____ 2. Keyboard   b. Preprogrammed, permanent memory

_____ 3. Modem   c. A CPU on a single chip

_____ 4. Program   d. Where data and programs are recorded and stored

_____ 5. RAM   e. Transmits data over standard telephone lines or fiberoptic cable

_____ 6. ROM   f. Let users enter information and change it into electronic signals the computer can use

_____ 7. Peripherals   g. Directs traffic within the computer

_____ 8. Microprocessor   h. An electronic tool

_____ 9. Monitor   i. The heart of the computer; does the actual processing

_____ 10. Input devices   j. Used for manually inputting letters or numbers

_____ 11. Memory   k. Transform electronic language into forms interpretable by humans

_____ 12. Arithmetic and logic   l. Consists of instructions to a computer on how to solve a certain problem or do a certain task

_____ 13. Control   m. Two or more computers linked together by cable or wireless means

_____ 14. Output devices   n. Working memory

_____ 15. Network   o. Output device for viewing data or graphics

Briefly explain the input–processing–output sequence of a computer.

_____

_____

_____

_____

Name _____

Date _____

Which occupation are you currently preparing for or do you hope to follow upon completing

your education and training? _____

Investigate and then list as many ways as you can (up to ten) in which computers are being
used in this occupation.

_____   _____

_____   _____

_____   _____

_____   _____

_____   _____

Describe a major occupational task now done by computers that could not be done, or could be

done only with great difficulty, without them. _____

_____

_____

_____

_____

_____

_____

How would you rate the need to understand and operate computers in relation to the
occupation listed? (Circle one.)

Absolutely Essential	**Essential**	**Desirable**	**Little Need**	**No Need**

Name _____

Date _____

Consult an encyclopedia (print version or on the Web) and write a short report on robots. You might want to mention such things as the history of robots, types of robots, how they work, and the impact robots are having on the workplace. Use this page to record your source and take notes.

Source

Encyclopedia title: _____

Volume No. _____ Article title: _____

Author(s) _____

Date of publication: _____ Publisher: _____

Place of publication (if on the Web, list the URL): _____

_____ Pages: _____

Notes

_____

_____

_____

_____

_____

_____

_____

_____

_____

_____

_____

_____

_____

_____

In this chapter, you learned about application software. One of the most popular types in business is spreadsheet software. It is used for budgeting, sales forecasting, income projection, and investment analysis. Engineers use spreadsheets to design bridges. Nutritionists use them in developing meal plans. Architects, mathematicians, teachers, scientists, economists, and historians all use spreadsheet software to analyze data.

1. Create the following spreadsheet.

	A	B	C	D	E	F	G	H
1	**Employee**	**SSN**	**Allowances**	**Hours**	**Rate**	**Gross Pay**	**State Tax**	**Federal Tax**
2	Chan, Ai-lien	000-56-5657	4	37.5	8.25		5	0
3	Han, Chi	000-23-4597	2	40	7.5		7	7
4	Smith, Andrew	000-98-4212	1	20	7		2	5
5	**Totals**							

2. Adjust the column widths to fit the contents of the columns.

3. Format Cells D2:D4 as Number with one decimal place. Format Cells E2:H4 as Currency with two decimal places.

4. Add columns for FICA and Net Pay (Columns I and J).

5. Format Cells I2:J4 as Currency with two decimal places.

6. Enter a formula to calculate each of the following in the appropriate cell in Row 2. Copy the formula to the two cells below.

   Gross Pay (Hours x Rate)
   FICA (Gross Pay x .0765)
   Net Pay (Gross Pay – deductions)

7. Use the AutoSum or SUM function to total the Gross Pay column. Copy the formula to the State Tax, Federal Tax, FICA, and Net Pay columns.

8. Add two rows at the top that say **SHEN CATERING** and **January Payroll.** Center the text and merge cells so this title and subtitle are centered over the columns.

9. Print your spreadsheet.

Name _____

Date _____

Spreadsheets are not just useful for making calculations. They can be helpful in reports, presentations, or anytime you need to present numerical data to others. Numbers arranged in rows and columns can be easier to understand than paragraphs of text. With the chart feature of spreadsheet software, you can create illustrations that can make the meaning of information even more clear.

1. Find some numerical data in a newspaper or magazine or on the Web. If you have access to the Web, a good resource is FedStats at ***http://www.fedstats.gov/***.

2. Create a spreadsheet from your data.

3. Use the chart feature of your spreadsheet software to make a chart that illustrates the data. Print your spreadsheet and pie chart.

4. In the space below, write a paragraph that interprets or comments on your data.

_____

_____

_____

_____

_____

_____

_____

_____

_____

CHAPTER 20

Entrepreneurial Skills

20.1 **Advantages and Disadvantages of a Small Business**
Objective: To identify and explain the advantages and disadvantages of being a small business owner

20.2 **Interviewing an Entrepreneur**
Objective: To interview a small business owner

20.3 **Entrepreneur Rating Scale**
Objective: To judge yourself in relation to traits considered important for success in business

20.4 **Planning for a Small Business**
Objective: To recommend steps to take and information to gather when planning for a small business

Name _____

Date _____

List as many advantages and disadvantages as you can (up to ten of each) of being a small business owner.

Advantages	**Disadvantages**
1. _____	_____
2. _____	_____
3. _____	_____
4. _____	_____
5. _____	_____
6. _____	_____
7. _____	_____
8. _____	_____
9. _____	_____
10. _____	_____

In your opinion, do the advantages outweigh the disadvantages? Explain your answer.

_____

_____

_____

Some people who do not want to operate a full-time business find that a part-time or seasonal business meets their needs. List as many examples as you can of businesses that can be successfully conducted on a part-time or seasonal basis.

_____

_____

_____

_____

_____

Name _____

Date _____

Identify a small business owner in your community to interview. Interview the person and fill in answers to the following questions.

1. Person interviewed:_____

2. Name of business:_____

3. What goods are sold, or what services are provided?_____

_____

_____

4. How many full-time employees do you have? _____ Part-time employees? _____

   People employed on an occasional basis (e.g., attorney, bookkeeper)?_____

5. What are the six most important job tasks that you perform?

   _____   _____

   _____   _____

   _____   _____

6. What type of educational background did you have before you started this business?

   _____

   _____

7. What type of work experience did you have before you started this business?

   _____

   _____

8. Which was more valuable, your educational background or your work experience?

   _____ Why? _____

   _____

   _____

   _____

   _____

(Continued on next page)

9. Have you taken any additional educational courses or training since opening the business?

   If so, what kind?_____

   _____

   _____

10. How many hours do you work each week? _____

11. How much vacation time do you have each year? _____

12. What three things do you like most about your business?

   _____

   _____

   _____

13. What three things do you like least?

   _____

   _____

   _____

14. If you had it to do over again, would you do the same things? _____ Why or why not?

   _____

   _____

   _____

   Use the additional space for your own questions and comments.

   _____

   _____

   _____

   _____

   _____

   _____

   _____

Name _____

Date _____

To be successful in business, you must honestly evaluate your strengths and weaknesses. Rate each of the following traits by checking off the appropriate response.

ENTREPRENEUR RATING SCALE

	Yes	Not Sure	No
1. I am a self-starter. I get things done.			
2. I like people. I can get along with just about anybody			
3. I am a leader. I can get most people to go along when I start something.			
4. I like to take charge of things and see them through.			
5. I like to have a plan before I start. I'm usually the one to get things lined up when our group wants to do something.			
6. I like working hard for something I want.			
7. I can make up my mind in a hurry if I want to.			
8. People can trust me. I do what I say.			
9. If I make up my mind to do something, I'll see it through.			
10. I am always careful to write things down and to keep good records.			

Source: Starting and Managing a Small Business of Your Own, *Small Business Administration.*

How many **yes** answers did you circle? _____ Based on your responses, are you the type to

run your own business? _____ Explain your answer. _____

_____

_____

_____

If you are the type to run your own business, what type of business might you start? _____

_____

_____

_____

Name _____

Date _____

Enrique is a work experience student who works at a local hospital. He thinks that he might someday want to have his own business traveling to people's homes and doing medical exams for insurance companies of people applying for life insurance. He has assessed his strengths and weaknesses and believes that he has the personality to be an entrepreneur.

1. What is the best way for Enrique to learn about this business? _____

_____

2. What are some basic skills (not medical skills) that Enrique should try to learn in school to prepare himself for this business?

_____

_____

_____

3. List eight types of resources for Enrique to get facts about the business he wants to start.

_____   _____

_____   _____

_____   _____

_____   _____

4. Can you think of some ways that Enrique might find out if there are potential customers for his business? Describe two possible sources of information.

_____

_____

_____

5. How can Enrique find out if this is a field in which growth is expected? Describe two possible sources of information.

_____

_____

_____

CHAPTER 21 Our Economic World

21.1 Economics Terminology
Objective: To name terms and concepts associated with economics

21.2 Circular Flow of Economic Activity
Objective: To explain and illustrate the circular flow of economic activity

21.3 Economic Growth
Objective: To understand concepts associated with economic growth

Fill in the correct word(s) in the spaces provided.

1. The study of how goods and services are produced, distributed, and used:

   _ _ _ _ _ _ _ _ _

2. Using natural resources, labor, capital, and management to provide goods and services:

   _ _ _ _ _ _ _ _ _ _

3. Any person-made means of production: _ _ _ _ _ _ _

4. The process of using goods and services: _ _ _ _ _ _ _ _ _ _ _

5. This is created whenever goods or services are bought or sold: _ _ _ _ _ _

6. The amount of goods or services available for sale: _ _ _ _ _ _

7. The willingness of consumers to purchase goods and services: _ _ _ _ _ _

8. The efforts of sellers to win potential customers: _ _ _ _ _ _ _ _ _ _ _

9. Type of economy in which people have no voice in economic decision making:

   _ _ _ _ _ _ _ _   _ _ _ _ _ _ _

10. Type of economy in which individuals and businesses can do more or less as they please:

    _ _ _ _   _ _ _ _ _ _ _ _ _ _

11. An economy that has features of both 9 and 10 above: _ _ _ _ _

12. The excess of income over expenditures: _ _ _ _ _ _

13. Exclusive control over the supply of a product or service: _ _ _ _ _ _ _ _ _

14. In a free enterprise economy, markets are: _ _ _ _ - _ _ _ _ _ _ _ _ _ _

15. A period of expanding economic growth: _ _ _ _ _ _ _ _ _ _

16. A downturn in the economy: _ _ _ _ _ _ _ _ _

17. A severe contraction in the economy marked by stagnant business activity:

    _ _ _ _ _ _ _ _ _ _

18. A sharp increase in the prices of goods and services: _ _ _ _ _ _ _ _ _

19. How much has been spent over budget or over what has been taken in: _ _ _ _ _ _ _

20. A collection of rights that allow people to make free choices:

    _ _ _ _ _ _ _ _   _ _ _ _ _ _ _

Name _____

Date _____

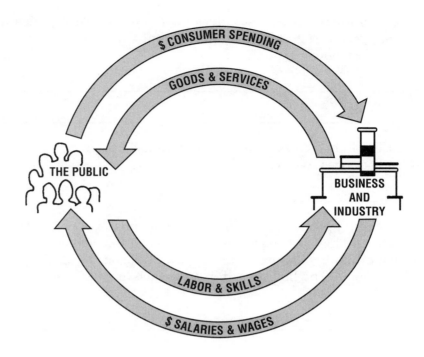

1. Provide a specific example to illustrate how the circular flow of economic activity shown actually works.

_____

_____

_____

_____

2. Place an X over one of the four half-cycles shown, thereby interrupting the "circular flow." Then explain what influence this interruption has on the remaining three half-cycles.

_____

_____

_____

_____

_____

_____

_____

_____

Name _____

Date _____

1. The United States' abundant natural resources have contributed significantly to its economic growth. Suppose you governed a country that was poor in natural resources. How could you still achieve economic growth?

_____

_____

2. You have read that the four factors of production are used to produce capital goods and consumer goods and services. Which factor of production does every person possess?

_____

3. You have read that capital goods are any person-made means of production, such as tools, machines, and factories. They are goods that can be used to produce other goods and services. Your school building is an example of a capital good. The building can be used over and over to educate people. The blackboard in your classroom is another example. List two more examples:

_____

_____

_____

4. Capital goods make people more productive. Use an example to explain why this is so.

_____

_____

_____

5. Where do businesses get the money to buy capital goods?

_____

_____

6. Suppose interest rates for borrowing money rise, as often happens in periods of inflation. What will happen to the demand for capital goods?

_____

7. "The American dream" has to do with economic opportunity and material success. What is another example of how our society demonstrates that it is generally pro-work?

_____

_____

CHAPTER 22 The Consumer in the Marketplace

22.1 Comparison Shopping
Objective: To compare the costs of selected products at three different types of retail stores

22.2 Advertising Techniques
Objective: To explain how a specific piece of advertising accomplishes four steps involved in selling

22.3 Sales Come-ons
Objective: To explain the message contained in various advertising statements

22.4 Used Car Prices
Objective: To obtain information about a used car from the *Official Used Car Guide* of NADA or its web site

22.5 Letter of Complaint
Objective: To write a hypothetical letter of complaint about a consumer problem

■ **Activity 22.1 Comparison Shopping**

Name _____

Date _____

For each type of product listed, select a popular brand and size. Then go to each of the three types of stores indicated and record the selling price for the products.

	Brand	Size	Convenience Store	Grocery Store	Discount Store
1. Toothpaste	_____	____	_____	_____	_____
2. Bath soap	_____	____	_____	_____	_____
3. Deodorant	_____	____	_____	_____	_____
4. Shampoo	_____	____	_____	_____	_____
5. Pain reliever	_____	____	_____	_____	_____
6. Antacid	_____	____	_____	_____	_____
7. Cold remedy	_____	____	_____	_____	_____
8. Juice	_____	____	_____	_____	_____
9. Granola bars	_____	____	_____	_____	_____
10. Dog food	_____	____	_____	_____	_____
Total			$_____	$_____	$_____

Give several examples and prices of store brands or generic products that you could purchase instead of a national brand.

_____

_____

The grocery store probably has some products sold in bulk that you can package yourself. Give several examples of the cost of bulk products compared to prepackaged products.

_____

_____

Generally you can save money buying generic brands and bulk products. Can you think of instances, however, in which generic brands or bulk products may actually cost more?

_____

_____

■ Activity 22.2 Advertising Techniques

Name _____

Date _____

Selling can be divided into four steps, listed below. Cut an ad from an old magazine that illustrates the four steps. Attach the ad to this sheet. Explain how the ad accomplishes each step.

1. Attracting the buyer's attention: _____

   _____

   _____

   _____

   _____

2. Getting the buyer interested: _____

   _____

   _____

   _____

   _____

3. Creating a desire to buy: _____

   _____

   _____

   _____

   _____

4. Encouraging the buyer to take action: _____

   _____

   _____

   _____

   _____

Name _____

Date _____

Even the most reputable store may exaggerate in its advertisements from time to time. What does each of these statements from ads really tell you or not tell you?

1. "Up to 50 percent off" _____

_____

_____

2. "Our lowest prices ever!" _____

_____

_____

3. "Storewide sale on selected items" _____

_____

_____

4. "Tremendous savings while quantities last!" _____

_____

_____

5. "Sold elsewhere for . . ." _____

_____

_____

6. "Ridiculous, giveaway prices" _____

_____

_____

7. "Items shown typical of merchandise available" _____

_____

_____

8. "Huge truckload sale" _____

_____

_____

Name _____

Date _____

Name a three- to five-year-old automobile and model that you would like to own (be realistic):

_____.

Obtain a recent copy of the *Official Used Car Guide*. Locate information for the auto listed and answer the following questions.

1. What is the average retail price for the car? _____

2. List three to five options for the car. How much would each add to the average retail price?

   _____   _____

   _____   _____

   _____   _____

   _____   _____

   _____   _____

3. What would be the total retail price of the auto with all of the options added? _____

4. Locate the mileage tables. How much would you add to the cost if your chosen car had

   20,000 miles less than the Trade-In value? _____

   How much would you deduct from the cost if your chosen car had 20,000 miles more than

   the Trade-In? _____

   _____

5. If you were trading in a car like the one listed, what would be its average trade-in value?

   _____

6. How can resources such as the NADA, Kelley Blue Book, or Edmunds web sites or print

   publications help you when shopping for a used car? _____

   _____

   _____

7. What other important factors, in addition to average listed price, should you consider in

   deciding how much to pay for a used car? _____

   _____

   _____

■ **Activity 22.5 Letter of Complaint**

Name _____

Date _____

Assume that on May 15, 20—, you purchased a TotalSound car CD player with a 12-month warranty from Hank's Stereo in Phoenix, Arizona. The CD player quit working on May 22 of the following year, one week after the warranty expired. It is defective, but the dealer will not fix it since the warranty is void. Write a letter of complaint to the manufacturer (TotalSound, Inc., 1403 Broad St., Lansing, MI 48901-3475). Use the return address 15 Echo Ave., Phoenix, AZ 85001-4493. The serial number of the player is 87492. Date the letter May 25.

_____

_____

_____

_____

_____

_____

_____

Dear Sir or Madam:

_____

_____

_____

_____

_____

_____

_____

_____

_____

_____

Sincerely

_____

Attachment

CHAPTER 23 Banking and Credit

23.1 **Managing a Checking Account**
Objective: To write and endorse a check, complete a deposit ticket, and record information in a check register

23.2 **Balancing a Bank Statement**
Objective: To balance an account statement

23.3 **The Cost of Credit**
Objective: To complete various questions and problems regarding the cost of credit

23.4 **Credit Application**
Objective: To practice filling out a credit application

■ **Activity 23.1 Managing a Checking Account**

Name _____

Date _____

Writing a Check

Fill out the check below for $47.16 to Chuck's Auto Service for repairs to your car. Use the date of April 8.

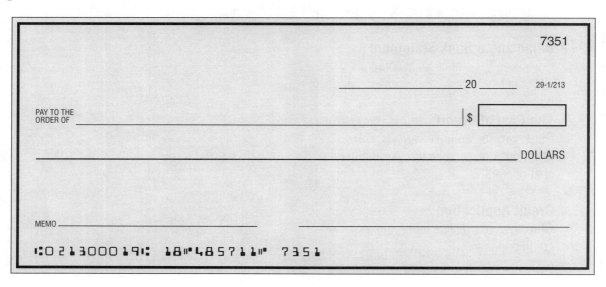

Endorsing a Check

Provide an example below of the three different forms of endorsement.

Blank Endorsement	**Restrictive Endorsement**	**Full Endorsement**

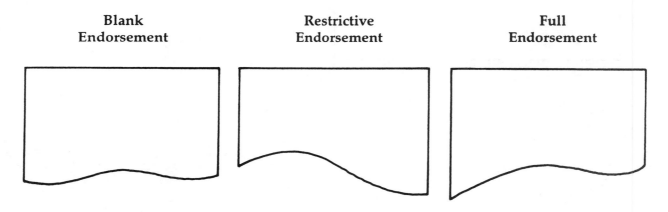

(Continued on next page)

Date _____

Making a Deposit

You want to deposit $89.75 in cash, as well as checks in the amounts of $23.18 and $37.85. Fill out the deposit ticket below using this information and the date of April 9.

DEPOSIT TICKET		CASH →			
		LIST CHECKS SINGLY.			
					29-1/213
_____ 20 ____		TOTAL FROM OTHER SIDE			USE OTHER SIDE FOR ADDITIONAL LISTINGS. ◀ ENTER TOTAL HERE.
		TOTAL ITEMS	TOTAL		BE SURE EACH ITEM IS PROPERLY ENDORSED.

⑆0 2 1 3 0 0 0 1 9⑆ 1 8 ‖ 4 8 5 7 1 1 ‖

DELUXE HD-14   CHECKS AND OTHER ITEMS ARE RECEIVED FOR DEPOSIT SUBJECT TO THE PROVISIONS OF THE UNIFORM COMMERCIAL CODE OR ANY APPLICABLE COLLECTION AGREEMENT.

Keeping a Checkbook Register

You have a checkbook balance of $235.46. Record the check you wrote to Chuck's Auto Service and the deposit you just made. Assume that you wrote two additional checks on April 10, to Record Mart for $12.37 and to Kavnar's Grocery for $31.53. Enter this information in the register below.

		RECORD ALL CHARGES OR CREDITS THAT AFFECT YOUR ACCOUNT.						BALANCE	
NUMBER	DATE	DESCRIPTION OF TRANSACTION	PAYMENT/DEBIT (-)	✔ T	FEE (IF ANY) (-)	DEPOSIT/CREDIT (+)		$	
			$		$	$			

■ **Activity 23.2 Balancing a Bank Statement**

Name _____

Date _____

Use the following information to balance your bank statement. The balance on the form should equal the balance in your checkbook register.

Statement balance: $437.62   **Checkbook balance:** $371.90   **Interest paid:** $1.82
Outstanding checks: **Deposits not credited:**   **Service charge:** $5.00
#273, $103.22 $37.46
#276, $14.34 $18.91
#277, $7.71

MONTH _____ 20 _____

THIS FORM IS PROVIDED TO HELP YOU BALANCE YOUR ACCOUNT STATEMENT.

**CHECKS OUTSTANDING
NOT CHARGED TO YOUR ACCOUNT**

NO	$	
TOTAL	$	

ENDING BALANCE SHOWN ON THIS STATEMENT $ _____

ADD ANY DEPOSITS NOT CREDITED IN THIS STATEMENT _____

TOTAL $ _____

SUBTRACT ANY CHECKS OUTSTANDING _____

BALANCE $ _____

CURRENT CHECKBOOK BALANCE $ _____

ADD ANY INTEREST PAYMENTS SHOWN ON THIS STATEMENT _____

TOTAL $ _____

SUBTRACT ANY SERVICE OR OTHER CHARGES SHOWN ON THIS STATEMENT _____

NEW CHECKBOOK BALANCE
should agree with $ _____

NOTE: Be certain to add to your register any interest paid and subtract from your register any miscellaneous charges (service charge, check printing charge, NSF charge, etc.) applied in the current statement period.

Name _____

Date _____

Answer the following questions related to the cost of credit.

1. The total dollar amount you pay for using credit is the _____ .

2. What types of charges may be included in the cost of using credit? _____

   _____

3. If you borrowed $2,000 for two years and paid $396 in interest, $12 for insurance, and a $5 service charge, how much was the finance charge you paid? _____What were your monthly payments? _____

4. If you borrowed $1,600 for a year and paid interest of $106, what was the total cost of the loan? _____How much was the monthly payment? _____How much interest was paid each month? _____

5. The percentage cost of credit on a yearly basis is the _____ .

6. Explain why the APR for a loan paid back in monthly installments is higher than the APR for a loan paid back in one lump sum. _____

   _____

Assume that you are going to borrow $5,000 and that the following three options are available. Look over these data and answer the following questions.

	APR	Length of Loan	Monthly Payment	Finance Charge	Total Cost
Creditor A	11%	36 months	$164	$893	$5,893
Creditor B	11%	48 months	$129	$1,203	$6,203
Creditor C	12%	48 months	$132	$1,320	$6,320

7. How much is the lowest possible monthly payment? _____

8. If you chose Creditor A instead of Creditor B, how much would you save on finance charges? _____

9. Suppose you are thinking of borrowing from Creditor C because it is offering a $50 gift certificate to new borrowers and the monthly payment is not much more than Creditor B's. Is this a good idea? Explain. _____

   _____

10. The cheapest credit is not to borrow money. List at least three things you should ask yourself before you borrow money or use sales credit._____

    _____

Name _____

Date _____

Complete the following sample credit application form.

APPLICATION AND CHARGE AGREEMENT

Please complete all sections for faster processing. Please print.

Personal Information

Name (First, Middle, Last)	Social Security No.

Address (Street, City, State, ZIP)	Home Phone (With Area Code)

Age	Driver's License No.	No. of Dependent Children	How Long at Address _____ Yrs. _____ Mos.	☐ Own ☐ Live with Parents ☐ Rent

Previous Address (Street, City, State, ZIP)	How Long at Previous Address _____ Yrs. _____ Mos.

Name (First, Middle Initial, Last) of Nearest Relative Not Living With You	Relative's Phone Number (With Area Code)

Relative's Address (Street, City, State, ZIP)	

Employment and Income

Employer	Type of Business

Business Address (Street, City, State, ZIP)	Position

Business Phone (With Area Code)	Monthly Salary	Length of Employment _____ Yrs. _____ Mos.

Name of Previous Employer (if Above Less Than One Year)	Type of Business

Business Address (Street, City, State, ZIP)	Position

Other Income Source (Optional). Alimony, child support, or separate maintenance income need not be revealed if you do not wish to have it considered as a basis for repaying this obligation.	Monthly Amount

Note: An applicant though married may apply for a separate account in his or her own name.

So your rights may be fully recognized, please indicate by a check mark if the following apply:	☐ My spouse will also use this account.	☐ My spouse's income should be considered in evaluating this application

Spouse's Name (First, Middle, Last)		

Spouse's Employer	Type of Business

Business Address (Street, City, State, ZIP)	Spouse's Position

Business Phone (With Area Code)	Monthly Salary	Length of Employment _____ Yrs. _____ Mos.
:		

Banking Facilities

Name of Facility (Checking)	Address (City, State)	Account No.
Name of Facility (Savings)	Address (City, State)	Account No.
Name of Facility (Loan)	Address (City, State)	Account No.

Credit References (if under a name other than Applicant's, please indicate)

Creditor	Address (City, State)	Account No.
Creditor	Address (City, State)	Account No.

CHAPTER 24 Budgeting, Saving, and Investing Money

24.1 Setting Financial Goals
Objective: To identify and evaluate your future financial goals

24.2 Record of Income and Expenditures
Objective: To maintain a record of your income and expenditures

24.3 Preparing a Budget
Objective: To develop a sample budget

24.4 Selecting a Savings Account
Objective: To collect and evaluate information regarding savings account options

24.5 Managing a Savings Account
Objective: To fill out savings account deposit and withdrawal tickets

24.6 Return on Savings and Investments
Objective: To calculate the return on various forms of savings and investments

Write down your personal financial goals for the next year and the next five years.

Goals for this year: _____

_____

_____

_____

Goals for the next five years:_____

_____

_____

_____

How much monthly income do you think you will need to be able to achieve your five-year

goals?_____

Will your present educational and occupational plans result in your having the income to

achieve your financial goals? Explain:_____

_____

_____

_____

_____

One of the best ways to ensure that you will be able to achieve your financial goals is to invest

in a good education. Do your five-year goals include saving money for your education? Explain:

_____

_____

_____

_____

_____

Use this form to keep a detailed record of all income and expenditures for one week.

RECORD OF INCOME AND EXPENDITURES

Week _____ 20____

Cash on hand _____

Date	Item	Income	Expenditure

End-of-week cash balance _____   Totals _____ _____

(Continued on next page)

At the end of the week, study the records. List at least three things you notice about your spending.

1._____

2._____

3._____

Summarize what you have learned about the pattern of your income and expenditures.

_____

_____

_____

_____

_____

_____

_____

_____

_____

Assume that you are married with one child and have a net monthly income of $_____.
Develop an estimated monthly budget using the following form.

HOUSEHOLD BUDGET FORM

Month _____ 20 ____ Estimated Income _____

Expenditure	Estimate	Actual	Difference (+ or -)
Savings			
Emergency reserve			
Goals			
Regular Expenses			
Rent or mortgage payment			
Utilities			
Insurance			
Auto payment			
Credit or loan payments			
Other ( )			
Variable Expenses			
Food and beverages			
Clothing			
Transportation			
Household			
Medical care			
Entertainment			
Gifts and contributions			
Taxes			
Other ( )			
TOTALS			

■ Activity 24.4 Selecting a Savings Account   Name _____

Date _____

Obtain information regarding passbook accounts from three different financial institutions in your area. Compare the institutions with respect to the following:

	Institution 1	Institution 2	Institution 3
1. What is the current interest rate?	_____	_____	_____
2. How often is the interest compounded?	_____	_____	_____
3. When is the interest paid?	_____	_____	_____
4. What is the APY?	_____	_____	_____
5. What is the minimum deposit?	_____	_____	_____

6. Describe any relevant service charges, rules, and restrictions.

Institution 1:_____

_____

_____

Institution 2:_____

_____

_____

Institution 3:_____

_____

_____

7. Based on the data you have collected, which of the three institutions has the best passbook savings account?_____

8. In addition to cost factors, what other factors should you consider before opening a savings account?_____

_____

_____

_____

Savings Deposit

You want to deposit $44.50 in cash and a check for $56.85 in a savings account (#4638-01). Fill out the deposit ticket below using this information and today's date.

SAVINGS DEPOSIT

DATE _____

▶ ACCOUNT NUMBER _____ ◯

NAME _____

	DOLLARS	CENTS
CASH		
LIST CHECKS SEPARATELY. BE SURE EACH ITEM IS ENDORSED.		
TOTAL DEPOSIT		

TELLER'S STAMP

SUPERVISOR _____

All unpaid items will be charged back to the depositor.

C - 153 500M 2/89-T

Savings Withdrawal

You want to withdraw $75.00 from a savings account (#4638-01). Fill out the following withdrawal ticket using this information and today's date.

SAVINGS WITHDRAWAL

DATE _____

PAY TO _____ **Or Bearer**

_____ **Dollars**

I HEREBY CERTIFY ALL PERSONS NAMED IN THIS ACCOUNT ARE STILL LIVING.

ACCOUNT NUMBER _____ ◯   ☐ CASH   ☐ CHECK

AMOUNT WITHDRAWN $

TELLER'S STAMP

CHECK NUMBER _____

_____
SIGNATURE

SUPERVISOR _____

_____
SIGNATURE

C - 153 500M 2/89-T

PASSBOOK MUST ACCOMPANY THIS ORDER.

■ Activity 24.6 Return on Savings and Investments

Name _____

Date _____

Answer the following questions related to the return on various forms of savings and investments.

1. What would be the return on a $1,200 savings account paying an APY of 8.5%? _____

2. You have a $2,000 certificate of deposit at a bank paying a 9% APY. How much money will you have at the end of 2 years, assuming that the interest is compounded annually? _____

3. How much interest would you earn in a year on a $500 savings account paying 6% interest, compounded quarterly? _____ What would be the APY? _____

4. How much interest would you earn in a year on a $3,000 savings account paying 7.5% interest, compounded semiannually? _____ What would be the APY? _____

5. You bought 100 shares of stock selling at $18.50 a share and paid a commission of $35. What was the total cost of the stock purchase? _____

6. You bought 100 shares of a company's stock for $32 a share. The company paid a quarterly dividend of $.48 a share. What was your annual dividend? _____ What was the rate of return, assuming the stock price stayed the same? _____

7. A stock that you bought at $27 a share increased in value to $42 a share. If you sold the stock, what would be your capital gain? _____

8. You bought 200 shares of stock for $25 a share and paying a $.20 quarterly dividend. You kept the stock for 2 years and sold it at $30 a share. Leaving out commissions, how much money did you earn? _____ What was your annual rate of return? _____

9. You bought a corporate bond for $1,000 that pays 7% interest quarterly. How much interest will you earn during the first quarter? _____

10. A $1,000 corporate bond may be sold for more or less than the issue price. If you bought a $1,000 issue paying 6.5% for $950, what would be your actual rate of return? _____

144

CHAPTER 25 Insuring Against Loss

25.1 **Insurance Protection**
Objective: To name the term or concept associated with various types and characteristics of insurance

25.2 **Which Type of Insurance?**
Objective: To identify the specific type of insurance coverage applicable in various situations

25.3 **Renter's Insurance**
Objective: To identify the need for renter's insurance and prepare a personal property inventory

25.4 **Automobile Insurance**
Objective: To investigate and describe auto insurance laws in your state

Complete the following word puzzle by filling in the correct term:

#										
1					I					
2					N					
3					S					
4					U					
5					R					
6					A					
7					N					
8					C					
9					E					
10					P					
11					R					
12					O					
13					T					
14					E					
15					C					
16					T					
17					I					
18					O					
19					N					

1. What people try to protect themselves against with insurance

2. A feature of major medical coverage that requires policyholders to share in the expenses

3. One of the three kinds of risks that people seek protection against

4. An amount that must be paid by a policyholder on a loss before the insurance company pays the balance

5. Insurance plans that usually provide more coverage and are less expensive than individual plans

6. A type of insurance that pays benefits to an individual who is out of work because of illness or injury

7. Costs resulting from illness or accident

8. Person to whom insurance death benefits are paid

9. Regarding life insurance, the amount of money that is paid in the event of the insured's death (two words)

(Continued on next page)

10. Something you should do with costs and coverages before you buy any type of insurance

11. Various types of damages for which you purchase home insurance

12. An alternative to traditional health insurance that covers preventative health care

13. A major, unexpected loss

14. The price of an insurance policy

15. A document that describes the terms of insurance coverage

16. Life insurance bought for a specified period of time

17. Another of the three kinds of risks that people seek protection against

18. The third of the three kinds of risks that people seek protection against

19. Another name for cash-value insurance

All of the following individuals have insurance coverage. Indicate which specific type of insurance applies in each case.

1. Emilio had surgery to remove a ruptured appendix.

   _____

2. Catherine's expenses were for hospital care, laboratory fees, and medications.

   _____

3. Gus had a very serious heart condition that kept him in the hospital for several months. His expenses were more than $20,000.

   _____

4. Paul was charged $450 by his doctor for medical visits while he was in the hospital.

   _____

5. Virginia's insurance pays for regular office visits and checkups.

   _____

6. Steve was ill and missed six months' work. His insurance, however, provided a portion of his normal wages.

   _____

7. Minnie has money withheld from her paycheck each week for group life insurance. She has a five-year renewable policy.

   _____

8. Daryl makes semiannual payments on a $50,000 life insurance policy. He receives annual dividends and is able to borrow money against the policy.

   _____

9. Tom will pay the same annual premium on his life insurance policy until he reaches age 55, at which time it will be paid up.

   _____

10. Diana and Tony have insurance that covers their house and its contents.

    _____

11. Janet lives in an apartment and has her personal property insured.

    _____

12. Arthur's car was damaged by a hit-and-run driver.

    _____

13. The hood of Helen's car was dented by a wayward golf ball.

    _____

14. Joji drove into the back of another car, injuring the driver of the other vehicle.

    _____

15. While backing out of the driveway, Beverly ran over her neighbor's new bicycle.

    _____

16. Alex bumped Carolyn's fender at the parking garage. The repair costs were paid by each person's insurance company.

    _____

17. Eloisa and her daughter ran off the road and hit a tree. Both required hospital treatment.

    _____

18. Scott was driving home when his car slid into a bridge. He had to pay a $250 deductible for repairs.

    _____

For whom is renter's insurance intended? _____

_____

_____

Assume that you and several of your friends plan to move into a furnished apartment in the near future. Complete an inventory of your personal property along with its estimated value. You may wish to group similar items together, such as clothes, jewelry, sporting equipment, and so on.

Item	**Estimated Value**
_____	_____
_____	_____
_____	_____
_____	_____
_____	_____
_____	_____
_____	_____
_____	_____
_____	_____
_____	_____
_____	_____

Total: $ _____

What would be the approximate annual premium for a policy covering this amount of property? (Allow an extra amount for things you will need to purchase.) _____

Why is it a good idea to photograph or videotape your personal property and to compile a detailed inventory of it? _____

_____

_____

_____

■ Activity 25.4 Automobile Insurance

Name _____

Date _____

1. Briefly summarize the financial responsibility law in your state: _____

   _____

   _____

2. What is the penalty in your state for violation of the financial responsibility law? _____

   _____

   _____

3. Does your state have a law requiring automobile owners to have liability insurance? If so,

   describe the requirements: _____

   _____

   _____

4. Does your state have no-fault automobile insurance? If so, describe how it works: _____

   _____

   _____

5. Below is a listing of the six types of automobile insurance coverage. For each type, answer yes
   or no regarding whether the coverage applies to the policyholder and/or to other persons.

	Whom the Coverage Applies to:	
	Policyholder	**Other Persons**
a. Bodily injury liability	_____	_____
b. Property damage liability	_____	_____
c. Protection against uninsured motorists	_____	_____
d. Medical payments	_____	_____
e. Collision	_____	_____
f. Comprehensive	_____	_____

6. If you have an old car that is not worth much, which of the above types of coverage might

   you do without? _____

   _____

   _____

CHAPTER 26 Taxes and Taxation

26.1 **Tax Terminology**
Objective: To name the term or concept associated with taxes and taxation

26.2 **Tax Rules**
Objective: To explain the purpose served by various income tax rules

26.3 **Tax Rates**
Objective: To illustrate differences between a graduated tax and a flat tax

26.4 **Filing a Tax Return**
Objective: To complete a sample Form 1040EZ tax return

Fill in the correct word(s) in the spaces provided.

1. The process by which the expenses of government are paid: _ _ _ _ _ _ _ _ _ _

2. A compulsory contribution of money made to government: _ _ _ _

3. Money that is raised through taxes to pay the cost of government: _ _ _ _ _ _ _ _ _

4. A tax that goes straight to the government: _ _ _ _ _ _ _ _

5. The tax you pay on money you earn: _ _ _ _ _ _ _ _

6. A tax that you and your employer pay to support Social Security: _ _ _ _ _ _ _ _ _

7. A tax that you pay on the amount of a purchase: _ _ _ _ _ _ _

8. A type of tax commonly paid on such items as gasoline, tires, and amusements:

   _ _ _ _ _ _

9. A tax assessed on a dead person's wealth and property: _ _ _ _ _ _ _ _

10. If someone leaves you money in a will, you may have to pay this tax:

   _ _ _ _ _ _ _ _ _ _ _

11. A tax paid on money or property given to you: _ _ _ _ _ _

12. A tax that increases in proportion to one's income: _ _ _ _ _ _ _ _ _ _ _

13. A tax for which the same rate applies regardless of income: _ _ _ _ _ _

14. Items such as alimony payments and individual retirement account contributions that may be
    deducted from your gross income: _ _ _ _ _ _ _ _ _ _ _ _   _ _   _ _ _ _ _ _ _

15. After subtracting the items in 14 above from your income, you are left with an:

   _ _ _ _ _ _ _ _ _   _ _ _ _ _ _   _ _ _ _ _ _ _

16. Items such as mortgage interest and property taxes that you are allowed to subtract from
    adjusted gross income: _ _ _ _ _ _ _ _ _ _ _ _

17. Set amounts for yourself and each dependent that you can subtract:

   _ _ _ _ _ _ _ _ _ _ _

18. The amount of income on which you pay tax: _ _ _ _ _ _ _ _ _   _ _ _ _ _ _ _

19. Reductions in the amount of income tax owed for child care and other expenses: _ _ _ _

   _ _ _ _ _ _ _

20. The crime of intentionally trying to avoid paying income taxes: _ _ _ _   _ _ _ _ _ _ _ _

21. The process of completing and submitting an income tax return: _ _ _ _ _ _ _ _

Name _____

Date _____

Many kinds of exemptions, deductions, and credits have been written into the tax law by Congress to accomplish certain purposes. Explain the purpose that you know or think might be served by the rules described in Items 1–7. Then answer Question 8.

1. Taxpayers who have children pay less tax. _____

    _____

2. An unmarried head of household pays less in tax than a single person. _____

    _____

    _____

3. Interest on a home mortgage is tax-deductible. _____

    _____

    _____

4. Taxpayers may deduct money contributed to charity. _____

    _____

    _____

5. Almost every working person is eligible to make contributions to an individual retirement account that can be deducted from his or her income tax. _____

    _____

    _____

6. A tax credit can be taken for child-care expenses. _____

    _____

    _____

7. You can deduct the cost of education required to keep your job and improve or maintain your skills. _____

    _____

8. A number of wealthy people and corporations are able to avoid paying taxes. What is your opinion of this? _____

    _____

The following table illustrates the relationship between a graduated tax and a flat tax.

TYPES OF TAXES				
	Graduated		Flat	
Income	Tax Rate	Tax	Tax Rate	Tax
$1,000	0	0	2%	$20
$2,000	0	0	2%	$40
$5,000	6.28%	$314	2%	$100
$7,000	8.51%	$596	2%	$140
$10,000	10.58%	$1,058	2%	$200
$20,000	15.65%	$3,130	2%	$400
$30,000	19.86%	$5,958	2%	$600
$40,000	23.84%	$9,536	2%	$800
$50,000	27.17%	$13,589	2%	$1,000

1. Answer these questions regarding a graduated tax.

   a. If your income was $2,000, how much tax would you owe? _____

   b. What is the tax rate for a person who earned $7,000? _____

   c. How much tax does a person who earned $20,000 have to pay? _____

   d. If your income increases three times, from $10,000 to $30,000, by how many times does

   your tax increase? _____

2. Answer these questions regarding a flat tax.

   a. If your income was $2,000, how much tax would you owe? _____

   b. What is the tax rate for a person who earned $7,000? _____

   c. How much tax does a person who earned $20,000 have to pay? _____

   d. If your income increases three times, from $10,000 to $30,000, by how many times does

   your tax increase? _____

3. What is the basic idea underlying a graduated tax? _____

   _____

4. What do you think is the basic idea underlying a flat tax? _____

   _____

5. Which type of tax do you think is fairer? Why? _____

   _____

Complete Form 1040EZ on the next page using the following figures: wages of $12,648, tips of $943, and $83 in interest income. You are not a dependent on your parents' return. Federal income tax in the amount of $1,248 was withheld. Use the table below to find the tax that is due (line 11). Sign your return.

At least	But less than	Single	Married filing jointly
		Your tax is—	
6,000			
6,000	6,050	904	904
6,050	6,100	911	911
6,100	6,150	919	919
6,150	6,200	926	926
6,200	6,250	934	934
6,250	6,300	941	941
6,300	6,350	949	949
6,350	6,400	956	956
6,400	6,450	964	964
6,450	6,500	971	971
6,500	6,550	979	979
6,550	6,600	986	986
6,600	6,650	994	994
6,650	6,700	1,001	1,001
6,700	6,750	1,009	1,009
6,750	6,800	1,016	1,016
6,800	6,850	1,024	1,024
6,850	6,900	1,031	1,031
6,900	6,950	1,039	1,039
6,950	7,000	1,046	1,046

(Continued on next page)

Name _____

Date _____

Department of the Treasury—Internal Revenue Service

Form 1040EZ

Income Tax Return for Single and Joint Filers With No Dependents (99) **2001**

OMB No. 1545-0675

Label
(See page 12.)
Use the IRS label.
Otherwise, please print or type.

L A B E L   H E R E

Your first name and initial | Last name

Your social security number

If a joint return, spouse's first name and initial | Last name

Spouse's social security number

Home address (number and street). If you have a P.O. box, see page 12. | Apt. no.

City, town or post office, state, and ZIP code. If you have a foreign address, see page 12.

▲ Important! ▲
You **must** enter your SSN(s) above.

Presidential Election Campaign (page 12)

Note. Checking "Yes" will not change your tax or reduce your refund.
Do you, or spouse if a joint return, want $3 to go to this fund? . . . . ▶

	You	Spouse
	☐Yes ☐No	☐Yes ☐No

Income

Attach Form(s) W-2 here.
Enclose, but do not attach, any payment.

1 Total wages, salaries, and tips. This should be shown in box 1 of your W-2 form(s). Attach your W-2 form(s). | 1

2 Taxable interest. If the total is over $400, you cannot use Form 1040EZ. | 2

3 Unemployment compensation, qualified state tuition program earnings, and Alaska Permanent Fund dividends (see page 14). | 3

4 Add lines 1, 2, and 3. This is your **adjusted gross income.** | 4

Note. You **must** check Yes or No.

5 Can your parents (or someone else) claim you on their return?
Yes. Enter amount from worksheet on back. ☐
No. If **single,** enter 7,450.00.
If **married,** enter 13,400.00.
See back for explanation. ☐
| 5

6 Subtract line 5 from line 4. If line 5 is larger than line 4, enter 0. This is your **taxable income.** ▶ | 6

Credits, payments, and tax

7 Rate reduction credit. See the worksheet on page 14. | 7

8 Enter your Federal income tax withheld from box 2 of your W-2 form(s). | 8

9a **Earned income credit (EIC).** See page 15. | 9a

b Nontaxable earned income. | 9b |

10 Add lines 7, 8, and 9a. These are your **total credits and payments.** ▶ | 10

11 **Tax.** If you checked "Yes" on line 5, see page 20. Otherwise, use the amount on **line 6 above** to find your tax in the tax table on pages 24–28 of the booklet. Then, enter the tax from the table on this line. | 11

Refund
Have it directly deposited! See page 20 and fill in 12b, 12c, and 12d.

12a If line 10 is larger than line 11, subtract line 11 from line 10. This is your **refund.** ▶ | 12a

b Routing number | ▶ c Type: ☐ Checking ☐ Savings

d Account number

Amount you owe

13 If line 11 is larger than line 10, subtract line 10 from line 11. This is the **amount you owe.** See page 21 for details on how to pay. ▶ | 13

Third party designee

Do you want to allow another person to discuss this return with the IRS (see page 22)? ☐ **Yes.** Complete the following. ☐ **No**

Designee's name ▶ | Phone no. ▶ ( ) | Personal identification number (PIN)

Sign here
Joint return? See page 11.
Keep a copy for your records.

Under penalties of perjury, I declare that I have examined this return, and to the best of my knowledge and belief, it is true, correct, and accurately lists all amounts and sources of income I received during the tax year. Declaration of preparer (other than the taxpayer) is based on all information of which the preparer has any knowledge.

Your signature | Date | Your occupation | Daytime phone number ( )

Spouse's signature. If a joint return, **both** must sign. | Date | Spouse's occupation

Paid preparer's use only

Preparer's signature ▶ | Date | Check if self-employed ☐ | Preparer's SSN or PTIN

Firm's name (or yours if self-employed), address, and ZIP code ▶ | EIN
Phone no. ( )

For Disclosure, Privacy Act, and Paperwork Reduction Act Notice, see page 23.   Cat. No. 11329W   Form **1040EZ** (2001)

CHAPTER 27 Social Security and IRAs

27.1 Social Security Coverage
Objective: To recall facts and characteristics regarding social security coverage

27.2 Administration and Financing of Social Security
Objective: To answer questions and solve problems regarding the two types of social security programs

27.3 Individual Retirement Accounts
Objective: To calculate the tax savings resulting from an IRA

Circle the letter T for each true statement and the letter F for each false statement.

T   F   1. An insured worker can retire at age 62 with full benefits.

T   F   2. The spouse of a retired worker can receive retirement benefits.

T   F   3. The age at which you can retire with full benefits is scheduled to be reduced from 65 to 62.

T   F   4. Retirement payments are the best-known program in the federal Social Security system.

T   F   5. Payments received by a dependent upon the death of an insured worker are called survivors benefits.

T   F   6. Survivors benefits may include both a lump-sum payment and a monthly benefit.

T   F   7. Only the spouse of a deceased worker can receive survivors benefits.

T   F   8. Payments made to an insured worker who is unable to work because of illness are called disability payments.

T   F   9. Disability payments are made only for physical disability.

T   F   10. Disability payments can begin one month after an individual becomes unable to work.

T   F   11. A spouse and other dependents are eligible for disability payments.

T   F   12. Hospital and medical insurance (Medicare) coverage begins at age 55.

T   F   13. Medicare pays 100 percent of all hospital expenses.

T   F   14. The medical coverage part of Medicare is an optional health insurance plan.

T   F   15. Unemployment insurance provides cash payments to workers who have lost their job.

T   F   16. Unemployment insurance benefits vary from state to state.

T   F   17. While receiving unemployment benefits, a worker can choose not to accept a suitable job offered by the state employment service.

T   F   18. Workers' compensation is to help individuals who become ill or injured as a result of their job.

T   F   19. Workers' compensation typically covers farm and household workers.

T   F   20. Workers' compensation laws are the same in all 50 states.

Name _____

Date _____

1. What is the difference between public assistance and social insurance programs regarding how they are financed? _____

_____

_____

2. Who administers the six types of social insurance programs? _____

_____

_____

3. The term *employment security* is sometimes used to describe unemployment benefits and workers' compensation programs. Explain why this is an appropriate label. _____

_____

_____

4. Answer the following questions in relation to the current calendar year. (Visit the Social Security web site at ***http://www.ssa.gov*** or contact a Social Security office to get up-to-date information.)

   a. How many work credits are required to be a *currently insured* worker? _____

   b. How many work credits are required to be a *fully insured* worker? _____

   c. How much do you have to earn a year to receive four work credits? _____

   d. How much is the current wage base? _____

   e. What is the current FICA tax rate for employed workers? _____

5. Compute the amount of FICA tax you would have to pay on the following annual earnings:

   $15,000 _____ $20,000 _____ $25,000 _____

   $35,000 _____ $50,000 _____ $75,000 _____

Name _____

Date _____

If you are qualified, you can set up an individual retirement account (IRA), contribute up to $3,000 a year ($4,000 beginning in 2005), and deduct the amount you contributed from your gross income when figuring your income taxes. Complete the following exercise to see how much you could save in taxes. Use a federal income tax table for the current year to find "Tax" and "Revised tax."

Taxable income:	$15,000	$20,000	$25,000	$35,000	$50,000
Tax:	_____	_____	_____	_____	_____
Taxable income with IRA contribution (Taxable income − $3,000):	_____	_____	_____	_____	_____
Revised tax:	_____	_____	_____	_____	_____
Tax savings (tax − revised tax):	_____	_____	_____	_____	_____
Actual cost of IRA contribution ($3,000 − tax savings):	_____	_____	_____	_____	_____

1. What does this exercise show regarding the tax-saving benefits of an IRA? _____

_____

_____

_____

2. How do our economy and our society benefit from the accumulation of IRA deposits?

_____

_____

_____

3. For young adults with most of their work life ahead of them, which type(s) of investment(s) (stocks, bonds, mutual funds, certificates of deposit) would be most appropriate? Explain why. _____

_____

_____

_____

CHAPTER 28 The Legal System

28.1 **The Nature of Law**
Objective: To identify terms and concepts associated with law and law enforcement

28.2 **Types of Courts**
Objective: To identify and explain the types and roles of courts located in your region

28.3 **Small Claims Court**
Objective: To describe the nature and role of small claims court

Complete the following crossword puzzle by identifying the correct terms having to do with law and law enforcement.

ACROSS

3. _____ attorney (lawyer who defends an accused person)

4. _____ law (defines rights and responsibilities under local, state, federal, and international law)

7. _____ attorney (lawyer who brings legal action against an accused person)

9. A hearing before a judge in which an arrested person is formally charged

11. _____ law (judge-made law)

12. Citizens who listen to the trial evidence and report their decision to a judge

13. A person who testifies at a trial

15. Money deposited with the court to guarantee a person will show up for trial

17. A court order authorizing a police officer to conduct a search, seizure, or arrest

18. Release of a convicted person under supervision and upon specified conditions

DOWN

1. A court order

2. The person against whom a court complaint or action is filed

4. The complaining party in a court case

5. _____ law (private law)

6. The person who presides over a court of law

8. A formal statement charging a person with an offense

10. A judge's decision

14. An order to appear in court

16. The body of enforced rules by which people live together

Name _____

Date _____

Answer these questions about types of courts found in your geographic area. You may need to do research at a library for the third question.

1. What is the name of the local court/lower court in your city or county? _____

    Where is it located? _____

2. What is the name of the general trial court in your city or county? _____

    Where is it located? _____

3. What is the difference between receiving a citation and being arrested? _____

    _____

    _____

4. In which U.S. district court area do you live? _____

    Where is the court located? _____

5. For each of the following situations, identify the type of court in your geographic area in

    which the case would be resolved.

    a. A person is arrested for speeding: _____

    b. A person is arrested for burglary: _____

    c. A person is charged with destroying a mailbox: _____

    d. A 14-year-old is charged with breaking a store window: _____

    e. A couple is adopting a baby: _____

    f. A person is cited for violating the city or county ordinance against burning leaves:

    _____

Name _____

Date _____

Obtain a copy of written guidelines regarding small claims court in your area. Answer these questions.

1. Why is small claims court sometimes referred to as the people's court?

   _____

   _____

   _____

2. Where is the small claims court located in your geographic area?

   _____

3. Provide three examples of complaints for which a suit might be filed in a small claims court.

   a. _____

   _____

   _____

   b. _____

   _____

   _____

   c. _____

   _____

   _____

4. What is the maximum amount of money that can be recovered from small claims court in

   your state? _____

5. Briefly outline the steps to follow in filing a suit in small claims court. _____

   _____

   _____

   _____

   _____

CHAPTER 29 Where to Live

29.1 **Housing Needs and Wants**
Objective: To consider your housing needs and wants

29.2 **Rental Agreement**
Objective: To explain the meaning of various statements often found in apartment leases

29.3 **Tenant Relationships**
Objective: To explain how to deal with various tenant relationship problems and situations

■ Activity 29.1 Housing Needs and Wants

Name _____

Date _____

1. How important to your overall lifestyle is a place to live? Explain. _____

_____

_____

_____

_____

2. Assume that you and a friend are going to share an apartment. List below those things that you need and want in housing. _____

_____

_____

_____

_____

3. Look through newspaper classified ads or on the Web for apartment rentals. How much does it appear that you might have to pay for an apartment that meets your needs and wants? What types of extras are often emphasized in apartment rental ads to attract young tenants? _____

_____

_____

_____

_____

4. Let us say that the type of apartment you need and want is not available or affordable. What things would you be most willing to give up? _____

_____

_____

_____

_____

The following statements were found in a rental agreement. Explain the meaning of each statement.

1. The Tenant accepts the premises in working order and agrees to clean and maintain the premises and to yield the premises at the end of the said lease period in the same condition, ordinary wear and tear excepted. _____

   _____

   _____

   _____

   _____

2. The Tenant agrees not to make any structural changes or cosmetic alterations on or about the said property without the previous written consent of the Lessor. _____

   _____

   _____

   _____

   _____

3. Upon execution of this agreement, the Tenant shall pay the Lessor a security deposit equal to the amount shown. _____

   _____

   _____

   _____

   _____

4. The Lessor and/or the Lessor's agent shall have the right to enter the premises at reasonable hours to make inspections or repairs. _____

   _____

   _____

   _____

   _____

(Continued on next page)

5. The Tenant agrees not to assign this lease without the written consent of the Lessor. _____

_____

_____

_____

_____

6. The Lessor is not liable for any damages to the personal belongings of the Tenant. _____

_____

_____

_____

_____

7. If the Tenant shall be in default of any of the covenants on his or her part, the Lessor shall

have the right to terminate the tenancy. _____

_____

_____

_____

_____

8. The Lessor shall have the right to terminate the tenancy where neither party is in default

upon delivering a notice specifying the Lessor's election to terminate. (month-to-month

rental) _____

_____

_____

_____

_____

Living in an apartment complex with dozens or hundreds of other tenants often presents difficult problems in tenant relationships. Explain how you would handle each of these situations.

1. When you come home from work, other tenants or guests are often parked in your reserved space. _____

    _____

    _____

    _____

2. Whenever you go to the pool to sunbathe, someone always seems to come over to chat. Most tenants are very nice, but you would really like to be left alone. _____

    _____

    _____

    _____

3. The couple down the hall cooks foods that are unfamiliar to you. Sometimes when you step out into the hallway, the smell almost makes you sick. _____

    _____

    _____

    _____

4. One of your neighbors is always borrowing an egg, a stick of margarine, a cup of milk, or the like. Very seldom does he pay you back. _____

    _____

    _____

    _____

5. Tenants are not allowed to have pets. However, you frequently hear a puppy barking in the apartment across the hall. _____

    _____

    _____

    _____

(Continued on next page)

6. You have lived in the apartment for several months but have not made any new friends. Everyone seems to be so busy. _____

_____

_____

_____

7. You often notice a person who seems to be watching your apartment. It makes you feel very uncomfortable. _____

_____

_____

_____

8. One of your neighbors has an infant. She often asks you if you would mind keeping your door open to listen for the baby while she runs an errand. _____

_____

_____

_____

9. Since your neighbors are not home, a delivery person asks if you will accept and sign for delivery of a small package. _____

_____

_____

_____

10. A new couple is moving into the corner apartment. They have been hauling their belongings all day and look absolutely beat. _____

_____

_____

_____

CHAPTER 30 Healthful Living

30.1 **Calorie Counting**
Objective: To record and analyze your calorie intake for a day

30.2 **Calorie Expenditure**
Objective: To complete questions and problems related to calorie consumption

30.3 **Learning to Relax**
Objectives: To answer questions about stress and meditation and to practice a simple relaxation method

30.4 **Healthstyle Self-rating**
Objective: To judge your own health habits

30.5 **Fitness Tests**
Objective: To evaluate your performance on five simple fitness tests

Keep track of everything you eat and drink (except water) for one day. List the foods and beverages. Record the number of calories for each item (for example, 6-oz orange juice, 83).

Breakfast	**Lunch**	**Dinner**	**Snacks**
_____	_____	_____	_____
_____	_____	_____	_____
_____	_____	_____	_____
_____	_____	_____	_____
_____	_____	_____	_____
_____	_____	_____	_____
_____	_____	_____	_____

Calories _____   Calories _____   Calories _____   Calories _____

1. How many total calories did you consume for the entire period? _____

2. What is your approximate caloric need, based on the National Academy of Sciences guidelines on page 455 of your text? _____

3. Is your calorie intake for the day above or below your needs? _____

4. By how much? _____

5. What percent of your calorie intake is composed of snack items?

   (snack calories ÷ total calories × 100) _____

6. Let us assume that you want to reduce your caloric intake. List five food or drink items (and their calories) that you could substitute for five of the high-calorie items listed.

   a. _____ instead of _____

   b. _____ instead of _____

   c. _____ instead of _____

   d. _____ instead of _____

   e. _____ instead of _____

This table lists the approximate number of calories per hour it takes to perform four tyes of activities. (The actual calories for individuals will vary.) Use it to answer the questions.

Activity Type	Calories	Examples
Light	105	Tasks done while sitting, standing, or walking slowly, such as reading, watching TV, working at a computer, grooming, washing dishes, doing laundry, sweeping, or shopping
Moderate	280	Carpentry, electrical work, stocking shelves, gardening, carrying a child, washing a car, walking (2.5-4.5 miles per hour), bike riding (leisurely), low-impact aerobics, water aerobics, bowling, or golf
Vigorous	420	Outside construction, shoveling snow, race walking, bike riding (10-11.9 mph), swimming laps (slowly), aerobic dancing, basketball, or tennis (doubles)
Strenuous	700	Carrying heavy loads, running, bike riding (>12 mph), swimming laps (moderate to vigorous), roller skating, tennis (singles)

1. About how many calories will be consumed in watching television for 3 hours? _____

2. If it takes you 2 hours to wash your car, how many calories will you consume? _____

3. Walking at 3 mph will consume how many more calories per hour than slow walking? _____

4. It takes about 3,500 calories to lose 1 pound of stored body fat. If you walk at 2.5 mph for 30 minutes a day, about how long will it take to lose 1 pound? _____ About how many pounds will you lose in 6 months? _____

5. If, in addition to walking 2.5 mph for 30 minutes a day, you reduce your daily calorie intake by 365 (10 french fries and a 12-oz root beer), about how long will it take you to lose 1 pound? _____ About how many pounds will you lose in 6 months? _____

6. If you reduce your calorie intake by 500 and increase your calorie use by 500 a day, about how long will it take you to lose a pound? _____

7. If you want to lose weight, what two approaches are recommended? _____

_____

8. If you go on a diet, what is the minimum number of calories you should maintain? _____ Why? _____

Name _____

Date _____

Use your textbook, an encyclopedia, or the Web as required to answer these questions.

1. How do you react to stress? _____

_____

_____

2. What is meant by the term *meditation*? _____

_____

_____

3. What types of bodily changes can be produced by meditation? _____

_____

_____

Try this simple relaxation technique (meditation). Sit or lie in a comfortable position in a quiet place where you will not be disturbed. Close your eyes, and silently repeat the word "one" over and over for a period of 10–20 minutes. Block out any other thoughts and concentrate on establishing a rhythmic pattern. Try not to move any muscles.

4. How do you feel after meditating? Describe any feelings or bodily changes that you noticed

while meditating. _____

_____

_____

_____

5. What do you do to manage stress? _____

_____

_____

6. Why is it important to be able to control stress? _____

_____

_____

_____

Name _____

Date _____

Circle the number corresponding to the answer that best describes your behavior (Almost Always, Sometimes, Almost Never).

	Almost Always	Some-times	Almost Never
EATING HABITS			
1. I eat a variety of foods each day, including fruit, vegetables, whole-grain breads and cereals, and dairy products.	4	1	0
2. I limit the amount of fat, saturated fat, and cholesterol I eat (fat on meat, eggs, butter, etc.).	2	1	0
3. I limit the amount of salt I eat.	2	1	0
4. I avoid eating too much sugar.	2	1	0
Eating Habits Score:			
EXERCISE/FITNESS			
1. I maintain my recommended weight.	3	1	0
2. I exercise for at least 30 minutes at least three times a week.	3	1	0
3. I do stretching and flexibility exercises for 15 to 30 minutes at least three times a week.	2	1	0
4. I use part of my leisure time participating in physical activities that increase my level of fitness.	2	1	0
Exercise/Fitness Score:			
STRESS CONTROL			
1. I have a job or do other work that I enjoy.	2	1	0
2. I find it easy to relax and express my feelings freely.	2	1	0
3. I recognize early, and prepare for, events or situations likely to be stressful for me.	2	1	0
4. I have close friends, relatives, or others whom I can talk to about personal matters and call on for help.	2	1	0
5. I participate in group activities or hobbies that I enjoy.	2	1	0
Stress Control Score:			

(Continued on next page)

Name _____

Date _____

	Almost Always	Some-times	Almost Never
SAFETY			
1. I wear a seat and shoulder belt while riding in a car	2	1	0
2. I avoid driving while under the influence of alcohol and other drugs.	2	1	0
3. I obey traffic rules and the speed limit when driving.	2	1	0
4. I am careful when using potentially harmful products or substances (such as household cleaners, poisons, and electrical devices).	2	1	0
5. I get at least 7 hours of sleep a night.	2	1	0
Safety Score:			

Interpret each section separately as follows:

10–9 **Excellent.** Your answers show that you are aware of the effect of this area on your health.

8–6 **Good.** Your health practices are good, but there is room for improvement.
5–3 **Poor.** Your health risks are showing.
2–0 **Failing.** You may be taking serious and unnecessary risks with your health.

Where do you go from here? Start by asking yourself a few frank questions:

1. Am I really doing all I can to be as healthy as possible?   **Yes   No**

2. What steps can I take to be more healthful?

_____

_____

_____

_____

3. Am I willing to begin now?   **Yes   No**   If the answer is no, why not?

_____

_____

_____

Adapted from Healthstyle: A Self Test. *U.S. Department of Health and Human Services, 1981.*

Name _____

Date _____

Perform each of the following five fitness tests. Have someone help you to keep time and to record information. Do not do the tests if you do not feel well or do not want to do them.

Arm Hang: Hang from the bar for as long as possible.

Your score in minutes and seconds: _____

Sit & Reach: Reach forward as far as possible while sitting (measure from crotch to fingertips).

Your score in inches you can reach: _____

Curl-ups: Do as many correct curl-ups as possible in one minute.

Your score in number of curl-ups: _____

Push-ups: Do as many push-ups as possible in one minute. (Note different style for men and women.)

Your score in number of push-ups: _____

Step Test: Step up and down on a 12-inch-high bench in rhythm for 3 minutes. Measure your heart rate after the exercise.

Your heartbeats per minute: _____

(Continued on next page)

177

■ **Activity 30.5 Fitness Tests**

Name _____

Date _____

Interpret your performance using the chart that follows. Find out whether you deserve a gold, silver, or bronze rating.

	Rating	Arm Hang	Sit & Reach	Curl-ups	Push-ups	Step Test
Female	Gold	1:31+	23+	46+	46+	to 79
	Silver	:46–1:30	17–22	25–45	17–45	80–110
	Bronze	to :45	to 16	to 24	to 16	111+
Male	Gold	2:01+	22+	51+	51+	to 74
	Silver	1:00–2:00	13–21	30–50	25–50	75–100
	Bronze	to :59	to 12	to 29	to 24	101+

How would you describe your overall fitness level (excellent, good, average, or poor)?

_____

If indicated, describe what you might do to improve your fitness level. _____

_____

_____

_____

Reproduced from the National Fitness Foundation.

CHAPTER 31 Responsible Citizenship

31.1 **The Nature of Citizenship**
Objective: To name terms or concepts
associated with citizenship

31.2 **Elections and Voting**
Objective: To answer questions
regarding election and voting
procedures and requirements in your
city and state

31.3 **Evaluating Propaganda**
Objective: To critique a piece of
propaganda

Complete the following word puzzle by filling in the correct terms.

						C				
2						I				
3						T				
4						I				
5						Z				
6						E				
7						N				
8						S				
9						H				
10						I				
11						P				

1. Good citizenship helps preserve this form of government.

2. Citizenship is acquired primarily by this process.

3. The legal basis for citizenship is contained in this document.

4. The special legal process of becoming a citizen

5. A person who holds the legal position of citizenship

6. People can serve the government by contributing to the national _____.

7. This type of citizenship activity involves producing efficiently and consuming wisely.

8. This type of citizenship activity involves preserving basic social institutions and adhering to the customs and laws of society.

9. A pledge of loyalty to the United States taken at a naturalization ceremony

10. This type of citizenship activity involves being informed on issues and voting during elections.

11. To share in the duties and responsibilities of citizenship

Answer the questions regarding types of elections and voting procedures and requirements.

1. Does your state have a **closed** or **open** primary election? _____

2. Does your state have a Presidential primary election? _____

    If so, explain how and when it is conducted. _____

    _____

    _____

    _____

3. What are the residency requirements regarding the following types of elections?

    a. National: _____

    b. State: _____

    c. Local: _____

4. Provide an example of a special election that has been held in your state or community.

    _____

    _____

5. Where do you go to obtain an absentee ballot in your city or county? _____

    Describe the procedure for casting an absentee ballot. _____

    _____

    _____

6. Why do you think that fewer than 40 percent of 18- to 20-year-olds vote in a general

    election? _____

    _____

7. Have you registered to vote, or do you plan to register? _____ Why or why not?

    _____

    _____

Propaganda appears in magazines, in newspapers, on TV, on the radio, and on the Web. You see it on billboards and bulletin boards. It arrives by mail and is passed out by people in the street. Obtain a statement of propaganda, or record notes about something you saw or heard. Identify the type of propaganda (pamphlet, magazine ad, television commercial, or other type) and explain how you became aware of it (arrived in the mail, picked up at the mall, etc.):

_____

Now, answer the following questions about the propaganda.

1. What is the primary message contained in the propaganda? _____

_____

_____

_____

2. Are you being urged to take some kind of action? _____ If so, what? _____

_____

3. What person or group is putting out the propaganda? _____

_____

4. Why do you think the person or group wants you to believe the propaganda? _____

_____

_____

5. What is the opposing argument or point of view? _____

_____

_____

6. In your opinion, is the propaganda good or bad? _____ Explain your opinion:

_____

_____

_____

_____

CHAPTER 32 Education for Lifelong Learning

32.1 **Evaluating Educational Alternatives**
Objective: To obtain descriptive information regarding an education or training alternative of interest

32.2 **Seeking Educational Information**
Objective: To practice writing a letter requesting information about education or training requirements and opportunities

32.3 **Apprenticeship Interview**
Objective: To rate yourself in relation to apprenticeship interview criteria

Name _____

Date _____

Identify a technical school, community college, college, or other education or training alternative in which you are interested. Contact the institution or use one of the sources of education and training information listed in Chapter 32 to obtain the information requested below.

1. Name of occupation for which training is desired _____

2. Name of program, major, or specialization _____

3. What type of degree, certificate, or other credentials will be received after completion of the

   program? _____

4. What are the entrance requirements? _____

   _____

   _____

5. How long does it take to complete the program? _____

   _____

6. How much does the program cost per year or total (specify)?

   ■ Tuition _____

   ■ Fees _____

   ■ Books and supplies _____

   ■ Room and board _____

7. Is any financial aid available? _____ If so, explain: _____

   _____

   _____

8. Does the institution provide job placement services? _____ If so, explain:

   _____

   _____

   _____

   _____

■ **Activity 32.2 Seeking Educational Information**

Name _____

Date _____

As part of Activity 14.4, you identified "Sources of Additional Information" for an occupation of interest. Select one of the sources and write an appropriate letter requesting information about education and training requirements and opportunities.

_____

_____

_____

_____

_____

_____

Dear _____

_____

_____

_____

_____

_____

_____

_____

_____

_____

Sincerely

_____

A person applying for entry into an apprenticeship program is required to complete an interview. A sample form used by interviewers to rate an applicant appears below. Fill out the form in relation to your view of yourself. Be honest in your ratings.

PART III. SUMMARY OF FACTORS (to be filled in by the Committee member during the interview)

Education: Survey of high school and college courses beyond those directly applicable to the trade

Poor background. Took minimum academic courses. Poor grades.	
Fair background. Some academic electives. Grades below average.	
Medium background. Average course electives with fair grades.	
Good background. College-prep or some college work.	
Excellent background. Extra subjects, college or post-high school with good grades.	

Remarks: _____

Physical Factors: Physical ability to perform requirements of the classification, lost time, health history, stamina, family health

Unsatisfactory because:	
Doubtful—verification needed:	
Satisfactory	

Interest: Desire to be a craftsperson, reasons for choosing this trade, knowledge of the trade, etc., interest in relevant hobbies

Total lack of interest (just wants a job)		Displays a real interest	
Little interest. Past associations show very slight interest.		Manifests a strong desire to be a craftsman	
Fair interest indicated by past associations and hobbies			

Remarks: _____

Attitude: Has he or she ever done any hard work? How was school attendance? Will he or she work under supervision? Has applicant participated in any organized groups, extracurricular activities, or sports? Examine past employment, school activities, and military records.

Unacceptable	Poor	Fair	Good	Excellent

Remarks: _____

Personal Traits: Appearance, assertiveness, sincerity, dependability, character, and habits

Unacceptable	Poor	Fair	Good	Excellent

Remarks: _____

After careful consideration of all factors, my grade for this applicant is (write in exact numerical grade such as 67, 83, or 95):

0	10	20	30	40	50	60	70	80	90	100

(Interviewer) _____ (Date) _____

EXPLORING OCCUPATIONAL INTERESTS

This part contains 12 occupational groups or clusters based on the Standard Occupational Classification system. The type of work performed within each cluster is explained, followed by a listing of specific occupations. The short descriptions of occupations are condensed from the *Occupational Outlook Handbook*.

Managerial 194

Science and Technology 199

Human Services 205

Personal and Public Services 210

Health Services 214

Arts, Communications, and Entertainment 221

Business and Marketing 224

Mechanical 229

Construction 234

Production 238

Natural Resources 242

Military 244

Part 2 begins with a brief explanation on pages 188–190 of how to interpret occupational information in the *Occupational Outlook Handbook* and a sample occupational description on pages 191–193. This information is also adapted from the *OOH*. This section concludes on pages 247 and 248 with a copy of the form contained in Activity 14.4, which is suitable for reproduction.

Interpreting Occupational Information in the *OOH*

The *Occupational Outlook Handbook* is best used as a reference; it is not meant to be read in its entirety. Instead, start by looking at occupation clusters. On the *Handbook* web site, you can access these clusters by using the buttons on the left side of each page. Look in the alphabetical index for specific occupations that interest you. On the web site, you can also search for a specific occupation using the box at the top of every page. For any occupation that sounds interesting, use the *Handbook* to learn about the type of work; education and training requirements and advancement possibilities; earnings; job outlook; and related occupations. Each occupational statement, or description, in the *Handbook* follows a standard format, making it easier for you to compare occupations.

Two other sections—"Tomorrow's Jobs" and "Sources of Career Information"—highlight the forces that are likely to determine employment opportunities in industries and occupations through the year 2010 and indicate where to obtain additional information. This section is an overview of how the occupational statements are organized. It highlights information presented in each section of a *Handbook* statement, gives examples of specific occupations in some cases, and offers some hints on how to interpret the information provided.

Unless otherwise noted, the source of employment and earnings data presented in the *Handbook* is the Bureau of Labor Statistics. Nearly all *Handbook* statements cite employment and earnings data from the Occupational Employment Statistics (OES) survey. Some statements include data from outside sources. OES data may be used to compare earnings among occupations; however, outside data may not be used in this manner because characteristics of these data vary widely.

Significant Points

This section highlights key occupational characteristics.

Nature of the Work

This section discusses what workers do. Individual job duties may vary by industry or employer. For instance, workers in larger firms tend to be more specialized, whereas those in smaller firms often have a wider variety of duties. Most occupations have several levels of skills and responsibilities through which workers may progress. Beginners may start as trainees performing routine tasks under close supervision. Experienced workers usually undertake more difficult tasks and are expected to perform with less supervision.

The influence of technological advancements on the way work is done is mentioned. For example, the Internet allows purchasers to acquire supplies with a click of the mouse, saving time and money. This section also discusses emerging specialties. For instance, webmasters—who are responsible for all technical aspects involved in operating a web site—constitute a specialty within systems analysts, computer scientists, and database administrators.

Working Conditions

This section identifies the typical hours worked, the workplace environment, physical activities and susceptibility to injury, special equipment, and the extent of travel required. In many occupations, people work regular business hours—40 hours a week, Monday through Friday—but in many other occupations, people do not. For example, waiters and waitresses often work evenings and weekends.

The work setting can range from a hospital to a mall to an offshore oil rig. Truck drivers might be susceptible to injury, while paramedics have high job-related stress. Semiconductor processors may wear protective clothing or equipment, some construction laborers do physically demanding work, and top executives may travel frequently.

Employment

This section reports the number of jobs the occupation provided in 2000 and the key industries where these jobs are found. When significant, the geographic distribution of jobs and the proportion of part-time (less than 35 hours a week) and self-employed workers in the occupation are mentioned. Self-employed workers accounted for nearly 8 percent of the workforce in 2000; however, they were concentrated in a small number of occupations, such as farmers and ranchers, child-care workers, lawyers, health practitioners, and the construction trades.

Training, Other Qualifications, and Advancement

After knowing what a job is all about, it is important to understand how to train for it. This section describes the most significant sources of training, including the training preferred by employers, the typical length of training, and advancement possibilities. Job skills are sometimes acquired through high school, informal on-the-job training, formal training (including apprenticeships), the Armed Forces, home study, hobbies, or previous work experience. For example, sales experience is particularly important for many sales jobs. Many professional and technical jobs, on the other hand, require formal postsecondary education—postsecondary career or technical training or college, postgraduate, or professional education.

In addition to training requirements, the *Handbook* mentions desirable skills, aptitudes, and personal characteristics. For some entry-level jobs, personal characteristics are more important than formal training. Employers generally seek people who read, write, and speak well; compute accurately; think logically; learn quickly; get along with others; and demonstrate dependability.

Some occupations require certification or licensing to enter the field, to advance, or to practice independently. Certification or licens-

ing generally involves completing courses and passing examinations. Many occupations increasingly have continuing education or skill improvement requirements to keep up with the changing economy or to improve advancement opportunities.

Job Outlook

In planning for the future, it is important to consider potential job opportunities. This section describes the factors that will result in growth or decline in the number of jobs. In some cases, the *Handbook* mentions that an occupation is likely to provide numerous job openings or relatively few openings. Occupations that are large and have high turnover, such as food and beverage serving occupations, generally provide the most job openings—reflecting the need to replace workers who transfer to other occupations or stop working.

Some *Handbook* statements discuss the relationship between the number of job seekers and job openings. In some occupations, there is a rough balance between job seekers and openings, whereas other occupations are characterized by shortages or surpluses. Limited training facilities, salary regulations, or undesirable aspects of the work—as in the case of private household workers—can cause shortages of entrants. On the other hand, glamorous or potentially high-paying occupations, such as actors or musicians, generally have surpluses of job seekers. Variation in job opportunities by industry, size of firm, or geographic location also may be discussed. Even in crowded fields, job openings do exist. Good students or well-qualified individuals should not be deterred from undertaking training or seeking entry.

Susceptibility to layoffs due to imports, slowdowns in economic activity, technological advancements, or budget cuts are also addressed in this section. For example, employment of construction craft workers is sensitive to slowdowns in construction activity, while employment of government workers is sensitive to budget cuts.

Earnings

This section discusses typical earnings and how workers are compensated—annual salaries, hourly wages, commissions, piece rates, tips, or bonuses. Within every occupation, earnings vary by experience, responsibility, performance, tenure, and geographic area. Earnings data from the Bureau of Labor Statistics and, in some cases, from outside sources are included. Data may cover the entire occupation or a specific group within the occupation.

Benefits account for a significant portion of total compensation costs to employers. Benefits such as paid vacation, health insurance, and sick leave may not be mentioned because they are so widespread. Though not as common as traditional benefits, flexible hours and profit-sharing plans may be offered by employers to attract and retain highly qualified workers. Less common benefits also include child care, tuition for dependents, housing assistance, summers off, and free or discounted merchandise or services.

Related Occupations

Occupations involving similar duties, skills, interests, education, and training are listed.

Sources of Additional Information

No single publication can completely describe all aspects of an occupation. Thus, the *Handbook* lists mailing addresses for associations, government agencies, unions, and other organizations that can provide occupational information. In some cases, toll-free phone numbers and Internet addresses also are listed. On the *Handbook* web site, links to non-BLS Internet sites are provided for your convenience (this does not constitute an endorsement). Free or relatively inexpensive publications offering more information may be mentioned; some of these may also be available in libraries, school career centers, or guidance offices or on the Internet.

Sample Occupational Description:
Data Entry and Information Processing Workers

Significant Points

Workers can acquire their skills through high schools, community colleges, business schools, or self-teaching aids such as books, tapes, or Internet tutorial applications.

Overall employment is projected to decline due to the proliferation of personal computers and other technologies; however, the need to replace workers who leave this large occupation each year should produce many job openings.

Those with expertise in appropriate computer software applications should have the best job prospects.

Nature of the Work

Organizations need to process a rapidly growing amount of information. Data entry and information processing workers help ensure this work is handled smoothly and efficiently. By keying text, entering data into a computer, operating a variety of office machines, and performing other clerical duties, these workers help organizations keep up with the rapid changes of the information age.

Word processors and *typists* usually set up and prepare reports, letters, mailing labels, and other text material. *Typists* make neat, keyed copies of materials written by other clerical workers or by professional or managerial workers. They may begin as entry-level workers by keying headings on form letters, addressing envelopes, or preparing standard forms on typewriters or computers. As they gain experience, they often are assigned tasks requiring a higher degree of accuracy and independent judgment. Senior typists may work with highly technical material, plan and key complicated statistical tables, combine and rearrange materials from different sources, or prepare master copies.

Most keyboarding is now done on word processing equipment—usually a personal computer or part of a larger computer system—which normally includes a keyboard, video display terminal, and printer. The system may also have add-ons such as optical character recognition readers. *Word processors* use this equipment to record, store, and revise letters, memos, reports, statistical tables, forms, and other printed materials. Although it is becoming less common, some word processing workers are employed in centralized word processing teams that handle the transcription and keying for several departments.

In addition to the duties mentioned above, word processors and typists often perform other office tasks, such as answering telephones, filing, and operating copiers or other office machines. Job titles of these workers often vary to reflect these duties. *Clerk typists*, for example, combine keying with filing, sorting mail, answering telephones, and other general office work. *Note readers* transcribe stenotype notes of court proceedings into standard formats.

Data entry keyers usually input lists of items, numbers, or other data into computers or complete forms that appear on a computer screen. They may also manipulate existing data, edit current information, or proofread new entries to a database for accuracy. Some examples of data sources include customers' personal information, medical records, and membership lists. Usually this information is used internally by a company and may be reformatted before use by other departments or by customers.

Keyers use various types of equipment to enter data. Many keyers use a machine that converts the information they key to magnetic impulses on tapes or disks for entry into a computer system. Others prepare materials for printing or publication by using data entry composing machines. Some keyers operate online terminals or personal computers. Data entry keyers increasingly also work with non-keyboard forms of data entry such as scanners and electronically transmitted files. When using these new character recognition systems, data entry keyers often enter only those data that cannot be recognized by machines. In some offices, keyers also operate computer peripheral equipment such as printers and tape readers, act as tape librarians, and perform other clerical duties.

Working Conditions

Data entry and information processing workers usually work a standard 40-hour week in clean offices. They sit for long periods and sometimes must contend with high noise levels caused by various office machines. These workers are susceptible to repetitive strain injuries such as carpal tunnel syndrome and neck, back, and eye strain. To help prevent injuries of these kinds, many offices have scheduled exercise breaks and have provided ergonomically designed keyboards and workstations that allow workers to stand or sit as they wish.

Employment

Data entry and information processing workers held about 806,000 jobs in 2000 and were employed in every sector of the economy; 509,000 were data entry keyers and 297,000 were word processors and typists. Some workers telecommute by working from their homes on personal computers linked by telephone lines to those in the main office. This enables them to key material at home while still being able to produce printed copy in their offices.

About 1 out of 3 data entry and information processing workers held jobs in firms providing business services, including temporary help, word processing, and computer and data processing. Nearly 1 out of 5 worked in federal, state, and local government agencies.

Training, Other Qualifications, and Advancement

Employers generally hire high school graduates who meet their requirements for keyboarding speed. Increasingly, employers also expect applicants to have word processing or data entry training or experience. Spelling, punctuation, and grammar skills are important, as is familiarity with standard office equipment and procedures.

Students acquire skills in keyboarding and in the use of word processing, spreadsheet, and database management computer software packages through high schools, community colleges, business schools, temporary help agencies, or self-teaching aids such as books, tapes, or Internet tutorials applications.

For many people, a job as a data entry and information processing worker is their first job after graduating from high school or after a period of full-time family responsibilities. This work frequently serves as a stepping-stone to higher-paying jobs with increased responsibilities. Large companies and government agencies usually have training programs to help administrative employees upgrade their skills and advance to other positions. It is common for data entry and information processing workers to transfer to other administrative jobs, such as secretary, administrative assistant, or statistical clerk, or to be promoted to a supervisory job in a word processing or data entry center.

Job Outlook

Overall employment of data entry and information processing workers is projected to decline through 2010. Nevertheless, the need to replace those who transfer to other occupations or leave this large occupation for other reasons will produce numerous job openings each year. Job prospects will be most favorable for those with the best technical skills—in particular, expertise in appropriate computer software applications. Data entry and information processing workers must be willing to continuously upgrade their skills to remain marketable.

Although data entry and information processing workers are all affected by productivity gains stemming from organizational restructuring and the implementation of new technologies, projected growth differs among these workers. Employment of word processors and typists is expected to decline due to the proliferation of personal computers, which allows other workers to perform duties formerly assigned to word processors and typists. Most professionals and managers, for example, now use desktop personal computers to do their own word processing. Because technologies affecting data entry keyers tend to be costlier to implement, however, these workers will be less affected by technology.

Employment growth of data entry keyers will still be dampened by productivity gains, as various data-capturing technologies, such as bar code scanners, voice recognition technologies, and sophisticated character recognition readers, become more prevalent. These technologies can be applied to a variety of business transactions, such as inventory tracking, invoicing, and order placement. Moreover, as telecommunications technology improves, many organizations will increasingly take advantage of computer networks that allow data to be transmitted electronically, thereby avoiding the reentry of data. These technologies will allow more data to be entered automatically into computers, reducing the demand for data entry keyers.

Employment of data entry and information processing workers will also be adversely affected as businesses increasingly contract out their work. Many organizations have reduced or even eliminated permanent in-house staff, for example, in favor of temporary-help and staffing services firms. Some large data entry and information processing firms increasingly employ workers in nations with low wages to enter data. As international trade barriers continue to fall and telecommunications technology improves, this transfer will mean reduced demand for data entry keyers in the United States.

Earnings
Median annual earnings of word processors and typists in 2000 were $24,710. The middle 50 percent earned between $20,070 and $29,500. The lowest 10 percent earned less than $16,410, while the highest 10 percent earned more than $35,410. The salaries of these workers vary by industry and by region. In 2000, median annual earnings in the industries employing the largest numbers of word processors and typists were as follows:

Local government	$25,710
State government	$24,850
Federal government	$23,890
Elementary and secondary schools	$23,300
Personnel supply services	$22,720

Median annual earnings of data entry keyers in 2000 were $21,300. The middle 50 percent earned between $17,850 and $25,820. The lowest 10 percent earned less than $15,140, and the highest 10 percent earned more than $30,910. In 2000, median annual earnings in the industries employing the largest numbers of data entry keyers were as follows:

Federal government	$27,260
Accounting, auditing, and bookkeeping	$22,310
Computer and data processing services	$20,480
Commercial banks	$20,410
Personnel supply services	$20,070

In the federal government, clerk-typists and data entry keyers without work experience started at $16,015 a year in 2001. Beginning salaries were slightly higher in selected areas where the prevailing local pay level was higher. The average annual salary for all clerk-typists in the federal government was $24,934 in 2001.

Related Occupations
Data entry and information processing workers must transcribe information quickly. Other workers who deliver information in a timely manner are dispatchers and communications equipment operators. Data entry and information processing workers also must be comfortable working with office automation, and in this regard they are similar to court reporters, medical records and health information technicians, secretaries, administrative assistants, and computer operators.

Sources of Additional Information
For information about job opportunities for data entry and information processing workers, contact the nearest office of the state employment service.

Managerial

In a small business, a single owner-operator generally performs all management functions. But, as the size and complexity of an organization increase, so does the management hierarchy. Functions such as accounting or legal services, which may be contracted out by small firms, are often performed internally by large corporations. Giant corporations contain several layers of management that are generally grouped into the three levels of supervisory, mid-level, and top management.

Supervisory, or junior, managers plan, schedule, and supervise the day-to-day work of employees. For example, a junior manager in a department store might supervise several salesclerks, keep records of inventory and sales, and be responsible for ensuring that adequate supplies of merchandise are on hand. Junior managers must be familiar with their firm's products or services, thoroughly understand work procedures, and have strong interpersonal skills.

Mid-level managers hold intermediary positions between supervisory and top management. They are always in charge of several junior managers. In a very large corporation that manufactures many products, a mid-level manager might be responsible for a separate division that makes only a few of these products. In a corporation that has a single pur-

pose, such as a supermarket chain, a mid-level manager might be responsible for all the stores in a region. Or mid-level managers might be responsible for a specific activity such as personnel, sales, service, or production.

Top-level managers include members of the board of directors, the chief executive officer (the president or chairperson of the board), and the vice presidents for major administrative units, such as marketing or financial operations. These executives establish the objectives of the organization and chart its future course. They must analyze and evaluate large amounts of information and monitor trends, technological change, and competition. They also coordinate the activities of various administrative units within their organizations and maintain lines of communication with mid-level managers.

Managerial occupations involve an interest in planning, organizing, directing, and controlling the major functions of an organization. Managers must be willing to accept responsibility and make tough decisions. As a group, managerial workers are older and more experienced than most other workers. A college degree is required for most managerial and administrative positions. The following occupations are included in the Managerial cluster.

Accountants and Auditors

Managers must have up-to-date financial information to make important decisions. Accountants and auditors prepare, analyze, and verify financial reports that furnish this kind of information to managers. The four major fields of accounting are public accounting, management accounting, government accounting, and internal auditing.

Administrative Services and Facility Managers

Administrative services managers work throughout private industry and government. They coordinate and direct support services to organizations as diverse as insurance companies, computer manufacturers, and government offices. Supervisory-level administrative services managers directly oversee supervisors or staffs involved in supportive services. Mid-level managers develop overall plans, set goals and deadlines, develop procedures to direct and improve supportive services, define supervisory-level managers' responsibilities, and delegate authority.

Advertising, Marketing, and Public Relations Managers

The fundamental objective of any firm is to market its products or services profitably. In large firms, advertising, marketing, and public relations managers coordinate these and related activities. *Advertising managers* oversee the account services, creative services, and media services departments. *Marketing managers* develop the firm's detailed marketing strategy. *Public relations managers* direct publicity programs for the firm and its activities.

Budget Analysts

Deciding how to efficiently distribute limited financial resources is an important challenge in all organizations. In most large and complex organizations, this task would be nearly impossible were it not for budget analysts. The major responsibility of a budget analyst is to provide advice and technical assistance in the preparation of annual budgets. Budget analysis is an integral part of the decision-making process in most corporations and government agencies.

Claims Adjusters, Appraisers, Examiners, and Investigators

Claims adjusters, appraisers, examiners, and investigators perform a wide range of functions, but their most important role is acting as intermediaries with the public. Insurance companies and independent adjusting firms employ adjusters, appraisers, examiners, and investigators to deal with the challenges they face, such as handling claims, interpreting and explaining policies or regulations, and resolving billing disputes.

Computer and Information Systems Managers

The need for organizations to incorporate existing and future technologies in order to remain competitive has become a more pressing issue over the last several years. As electronic commerce becomes more common, how and when companies use technology are critical issues. Computer and information systems managers play a vital role in the technological direction of their organizations. They do everything from constructing the business plan to overseeing network and Internet operations.

Construction and Building Inspectors

Construction and building inspectors examine the construction, alteration, or repair of buildings, highways and streets, sewer and water systems, dams, bridges, and other structures to ensure compliance with building codes and ordinances, zoning regulations, and contract specifications. Building codes and standards are the primary means by which building construction is regulated in the United States to ensure the health and safety of the general public.

Construction Managers

Construction managers plan and direct construction projects. They may have job titles such as *constructor, construction superintendent, general superintendent, project engineer, project manager, general construction manager,* or *executive construction manager.* Construction managers may be owners or salaried employees of a construction management or contracting firm. They may also be under contract to or salaried employees of the owner, developer, contractor, or management firm overseeing the construction project.

Cost Estimators

Being able to predict the cost of future projects is vital to the economic survival of any business. Cost estimators develop this information for owners, managers, and government. The information is used in making bids for contracts, in determining if a new product will be profitable, or in determining if the government is getting good value for the taxpayer's money.

Education Administrators

Smooth operation of an educational institution requires competent administrators. Education administrators provide direction, leadership, and day-to-day management of educational activities in schools, preschools and day-care centers, colleges and universities, businesses, correctional institutions, museums, and job training and community service organizations.

Engineering and Natural Sciences Managers

Engineering and natural sciences managers plan, coordinate, and direct research, design, and production activities. They may supervise engineers, scientists, and technicians, along with support personnel. These managers use advanced technical knowledge of engineering and science to oversee a variety of activities. They determine scientific and technical goals within broad outlines provided by top executives.

Financial Analysts and Personal Financial Advisors

Financial analysts and personal financial advisors provide investment analysis and guidance to businesses and individuals to help them with their investment decisions. They gather financial information, analyze it, and make recommendations. Their job duties differ, however, because of the type of investment information they provide and the clients they work for. *Financial analysts* assess the economic performance of companies and industries for firms and institutions with money to invest. *Personal financial advisors* generally assess the financial needs of individuals, providing them a wide range of options.

Financial Managers

Practically every firm has one or more financial managers (*treasurer, controller, cash manager*) who prepare the financial reports required by the firm to conduct its operations and to satisfy tax and regulatory requirements. Financial managers also oversee the flow of cash and financial instruments and develop information to assess the present and future financial status of the firm.

Food Service Managers

The daily responsibilities of many food service managers can often be as complicated as some of the meals prepared by a fine chef. In addition to the traditional duties of selecting and pricing menu items, using food and other supplies efficiently, and achieving quality in food preparation and service, managers now are responsible for a growing number of administrative and human resource tasks. For example, managers must carefully find and evaluate new ways of recruiting employees in a tight job market.

Funeral Directors

Funeral directors, also called *morticians* or *undertakers*, arrange and direct the details of funerals. These include removal of the deceased to a mortuary, preparation of the remains, performance of a ceremony that honors the deceased and addresses the spiritual needs of the living, and burial or transfer of the remains. Most funeral directors are also trained, licensed, and practicing embalmers.

Human Resources, Training, and Labor Relations Managers and Specialists

Attracting the most qualified employees and matching them to the jobs for which they are best suited are important for the success of any organization. However, many enterprises are too large to permit close contact between top management and employees. Human resources, training, and labor relations managers and specialists provide this link. Dealing with people is an essential part of the job.

Industrial Production Managers

Each day we consume products made in thousands of factories across the country. Most factories share a similar organizational structure. That is, production workers operate industrial machinery and equipment to produce goods. First-line supervisors oversee these workers. Directing the work of first-line supervisors and coordinating production are the responsibilities of industrial production managers.

Insurance Underwriters

Insurance companies protect individuals and organizations from financial loss by assuming billions of dollars in risks each year. Underwriters are needed to identify and calculate the risk of loss from policyholders, establish appropriate premium rates, and write policies that cover these risks.

Loan Counselors and Officers

Banks and financial institutions need up-to-date information on companies and individuals applying for loans and credit. Customers and clients provide this information to the financial institutions. *Loan officers* prepare, analyze, and verify loan applications, make decisions regarding the extension of credit, and help borrowers fill out loan applications. *Loan counselors* help consumers with low income or a poor credit history qualify for credit.

Lodging Managers

A comfortable room, good food, and a helpful staff can make being away from home an enjoyable experience for both vacationing families and business travelers. While most lodging managers work in traditional hotels and motels, some work in other lodging establishments, such as camps, inns, boardinghouses, dude ranches, and recreational resorts.

Management Analysts

Management analysts and consultants help organizations solve problems in areas such as structure, efficiency, purchasing, and profits. Individuals who work in government agencies are called *management analysts*. Those who work in private business are usually called *management consultants*. In general, analysts and consultants collect, review, and analyze information. They also make recommendations and often assist in the implementation of their proposals.

Medical and Health Services Managers

Health care is a business. Like every other business, it needs good management to keep it running smoothly. The term *medical and health services manager* encompasses all individuals who plan, direct, coordinate, and supervise the delivery of health care. Medical and health services managers include specialists and generalists. Specialists are in charge of specific clinical departments or services, while generalists manage or help to manage an entire facility or system.

Property, Real Estate, and Community Association Managers

To businesses and investors, properly managed real estate is a potential source of income and profits, and to homeowners, it is a way to preserve and enhance resale values. Property, real estate, and community association managers maintain and increase the value of real estate investments. *Property and real estate managers* oversee the performance of income-producing commercial or residential properties and ensure that real estate investments achieve their expected revenues. *Community association managers* manage the common property and services of condominiums, cooperatives, and planned communities.

Purchasing Managers, Buyers, and Purchasing Agents

Purchasing managers, buyers, and purchasing agents seek to obtain the highest-quality merchandise at the lowest possible cost for their employers. In general, *purchasers* buy goods and services for their company or organization, whereas *buyers* typically buy items for resale. Purchasers and buyers determine which commodity or service is best, choose the suppliers of the product or service, negotiate the lowest price, and award contracts that ensure that the correct amount of the product or type of service is received at the appropriate time.

Tax Examiners, Collectors, and Revenue Agents

Taxes are one of the certainties of life. And, as long as governments collect taxes, there will be jobs for tax examiners, collectors, and revenue agents. These workers ensure that governments obtain revenues from businesses and citizens by reviewing tax returns, conducting audits, identifying taxes payable, and collecting overdue tax dollars.

Top Executives

All organizations have specific goals and objectives. Top executives devise strategies and formulate policies to ensure these goals and objectives are met. Although they have a wide range of titles, such as *chief executive officer*, *board chair*, *president*, *vice president*, *school superintendent*, *county administrator*, and *tax commissioner*, all formulate policies and direct the operations of businesses and corporations, nonprofit institutions, governments, and other organizations.

Science and Technology

Have you ever gazed at the stars on a clear night and wondered what is out there? Have you ever asked yourself what causes volcanic eruptions, earthquakes, or tidal waves? Or wondered how an airplane the length of a football field can lift off the ground and fly?

People have always wanted to understand the universe. The work of scientists, engineers, technicians, and related occupations has grown out of this desire to know. The scientist gathers knowledge that the engineer applies to solving problems. Technicians assist scientists and engineers in their work.

Science and technology occupations involve discovering, collecting, and analyzing information. They also involve applying knowledge to theoretical and practical problems. Some occupations in this group work primarily with scientific and mechanical equipment and procedures. The Science and Technology cluster includes occupations organized into three groups.

ENGINEERS, ARCHITECTS, AND SURVEYORS

This group includes occupations concerned with the application of architectural and engineering principles in the design and construction of buildings, equipment and processing systems, highways and roads, and utilization of land areas.

Architects, engineers, and surveyors often work together on building projects. Architects design the building. They concentrate on the visual appearance as well as the needs of the occupants. Engineers design the building's mechanical, heating, and electrical systems. Surveyors lay out the boundaries of the building and the land it occupies. The following occupations are included in the Engineers, Architects, and Surveyors group.

Architects

Architects provide services to individuals and organizations planning a building project. They design office and apartment buildings, schools, churches, factories, hospitals, houses, and airport terminals. In addition to designing buildings, architects may advise on the selection of building sites, prepare cost and land-use studies, and do long-range planning for land development.

Engineers

Engineers apply the theories and principles of science and mathematics to the solution of practical technical problems. Often their work is the link between a scientific discovery and its application. Most engineers specialize. More than 25 major specialties are recognized by professional societies, and the major branches have numerous subdivisions. Some examples include structural, environmental, and transportation engineering, which are subdivisions of civil engineering; and ceramic, metallurgical, and polymer engineering, which are subdivisions of materials engineering. Engineers also may specialize in one industry, such as motor vehicles, or in one field of technology, such as turbines or semiconductor materials.

Landscape Architects

Everyone enjoys attractively designed residential areas, public parks, college campuses, shopping centers, golf courses, parkways, and industrial parks. Landscape architects design such areas so that they are beautiful, functional, and environmentally appropriate. Many types of organizations—from real estate development firms starting new projects to municipalities constructing airports or parks—hire landscape architects, who often are involved with the development of a site from its conception.

Surveyors and Related Workers

Measuring and mapping the earth's surface are the responsibilities of several different types of workers. Traditional *land surveyors* establish official land, air-space, and water boundaries. They write descriptions of land for deeds, leases, and other legal documents; define air space for airports; and measure construction and mineral sites. *Cartographers* compile geographic, political, and cultural information and prepare maps of large areas. *Photogrammetrists* measure and analyze aerial photographs to prepare detailed maps and drawings.

NATURAL SCIENTISTS AND MATHEMATICIANS

This group includes occupations concerned with the application of scientific and mathematical knowledge to the conducting of research and development and related activities. Natural and mathematical scientists seek knowledge of the physical world through observation, study, and experimentation. The knowledge gained through these research activities is used to develop new products, increase productivity, protect the environment, and improve health care.

Three subgroups make up this broad occupational field. Physical scientists study the nature of matter and energy, both on earth and in the rest of the universe. They also study how physical processes influence the earth and its atmosphere. Life scientists study living organisms and life processes. Computer and mathematical scientists study mathematics and use it as a tool to solve practical and theoretical problems in business, science, and engineering. The following occupations are included in the Natural Scientists and Mathematicians group.

Actuaries

Actuaries assemble and analyze data to estimate probabilities of an event taking place, such as death, sickness, injury, disability, or property loss. They also make price decisions and formulate investment strategies. In addition, some actuaries design insurance, financial, and pension plans and ensure that these plans are maintained on a sound financial basis. Most of these workers specialize in life and health or property and casualty insurance; others work primarily in finance or employee benefits.

Agricultural and Food Scientists

The work of agricultural and food scientists plays an important part in maintaining the nation's food supply by ensuring agricultural productivity and the safety of the food supply. Agricultural scientists study farm crops and animals and develop ways of improving their quantity and quality. They look for ways to improve crop yield with less labor, control pests and weeds more safely and effectively, and conserve soil and water. They research methods of converting raw agricultural commodities into attractive and healthy food products for consumers.

Atmospheric Scientists

Atmospheric scientists, commonly called *meteorologists*, study the atmosphere's physical characteristics, motions, and processes and the way it affects the rest of our environment. The best-known application of this knowledge is in forecasting the weather. However, weather information and meteorological research are also applied in air pollution control, agriculture, air and sea transportation, defense, and the study of trends in the earth's climate, such as global warming, droughts, or ozone depletion.

Biological and Medical Scientists

Biological and medical scientists study living organisms and their relationship to their environment. They research problems dealing with life processes. Most specialize in some area of biology such as zoology (the study of animals) or microbiology (the study of microscopic organisms). Many biological scientists and virtually all medical scientists work in research and development.

Chemists and Materials Scientists

Chemists and materials scientists study and work with chemicals to learn more about them and find new ways that they may be useful to people. Chemical research has led to the discovery and development of new and improved synthetic fibers, paints, adhesives, drugs, cosmetics, electronic components, lubricants, and thousands of other products. Chemists and materials scientists also develop processes that save energy and reduce pollution, such as improved oil refining and petrochemical processing methods.

Computer Software Engineers

The tasks performed by workers known as computer software engineers are changing rapidly, as technology changes, new areas of specialization arise, and employers modify their procedures and preferences. Computer software engineers apply the principles and techniques of computer science, engineering, and mathematical analysis to the design, development, testing, and evaluation of the software and systems that enable computers to perform their many applications.

Conservation Scientists and Foresters

Forests and rangelands supply wood products, livestock forage, minerals, and water; serve as sites for recreational activities; and provide habitats for wildlife. Conservation scientists and foresters manage, develop, use, and help to protect these and other natural resources. Foresters and conservation scientists often specialize in one area, such as forest resource management, urban forestry, wood technology, or forest economics.

Environmental Scientists and Geoscientists

Environmental scientists and geoscientists use their knowledge of the physical makeup and history of the earth to locate water, mineral, and energy resources; protect the environment; predict future geologic hazards; and offer advice on construction and land use projects. *Environmental scientists* conduct research to identify and abate or eliminate sources of pollutants that affect people, wildlife, and their environments. *Geoscientists* study the composition, structure, and other physical aspects of the earth.

Mathematicians

Mathematics is one of the oldest and most basic sciences. Mathematical work falls into two broad classes. *Theoretical mathematicians* seek to increase basic knowledge without necessarily considering its practical use. *Applied mathematicians* use mathematics to develop theories and techniques such as mathematical modeling and computational methods. These are used to solve practical problems in business, government, and engineering and in the physical, life, and social sciences.

Operations Research Analysts

Operations research analysts help organizations plan and operate in the most efficient and effective manner. They accomplish this by applying the scientific method and mathematical principles to organizational problems. They help managers evaluate alternatives and choose the course of action that best suits the organization. Operations research analysts are problem solvers.

Physicists and Astronomers

Physicists attempt to discover basic principles governing the structure and behavior of matter, the generation and transfer of energy, and the interaction of matter and energy. Astronomy is sometimes considered a subfield of physics. *Astronomers* use the principles of physics and mathematics to learn about the fundamental nature of the universe and the sun, moon, planets, stars, and galaxies.

Statisticians

Statistics deals with the collection, analysis, and presentation of numerical data. Statisticians design, carry out, and interpret the numerical results of surveys and experiments. They use statistical techniques to predict population growth or economic conditions, develop quality control tests for manufactured products, and assess the nature of environmental problems.

Systems Analysts, Computer Scientists, and Database Administrators

The rapid spread of computers and information technology has generated a need for highly trained workers to design and develop new hardware and software systems and to incorporate new technologies. These workers—*computer systems analysts*, *computer scientists*, and *database administrators*—include a wide range of computer specialists. Job tasks and occupational titles used to describe these workers continue to evolve, reflecting new areas of specialization and changes in technology, as well as the preferences and practices of employers.

TECHNOLOGISTS AND TECHNICIANS

Workers in this group perform much of the detailed technical work necessary in engineering, scientific, broadcasting, manufacturing, and other types of activities. Technologists and technicians perform the day-to-day tasks needed to carry out a project or run an operation. Many workers in this group operate complex electronic and mechanical equipment and vehicles. They are employed in nearly every industry where technical assistance in a specialized area is needed. They are usually part of a team that is engaged in a particular project or operation. The following occupations are included in the Technologists and Technicians group.

Aircraft Pilots and Flight Engineers

Pilots are highly trained professionals who fly airplanes and helicopters to carry out a wide variety of tasks. Although four out of five are *airline pilots, copilots,* and *flight engineers* who transport passengers and cargo, others are *commercial pilots* involved in more unusual tasks, such as dusting crops, spreading seed for reforestation, testing aircraft, and flying passengers and cargo to areas not serviced by regular airlines.

Air Traffic Controllers

The air traffic control system is a vast network of people and equipment that ensures the safe operation of commercial and private aircraft. Air traffic controllers coordinate the movement of air traffic to make certain that planes stay a safe distance apart. Their immediate concern is safety, but controllers also must direct planes efficiently to minimize delays. Some regulate airport traffic; others regulate flights between airports.

Broadcast and Sound Engineering Technicians and Radio Operators

Broadcast and sound engineering technicians install, test, repair, set up, and operate the electronic equipment used to record and transmit radio and television programs, cable programs, and motion pictures. They work with television cameras, microphones, tape recorders, lighting, equipment used to produce sound effects, transmitters, antennas, and other equipment. Some broadcast and sound engineering technicians produce movie soundtracks in motion picture production studios, control the sound of live events such as concerts, or record music in a recording studio.

Computer Programmers

Computer programmers write, update, and maintain the detailed instructions (called programs or software) that computers must execute. *Applications programmers* are oriented toward business, engineering, or science. They write software to handle specific jobs, such as a program used in an inventory control system or to guide a missile after it has been fired. *Systems programmers* maintain the software that controls the operation of the entire computer system.

Computer Support Specialists and Systems Administrators

The explosion of computer use has created a great demand for specialists to provide advice to users, as well as day-to-day administration, maintenance, and support of computer systems and networks. *Computer support specialists* provide technical assistance, support, and advice to customers and other users. This group includes *technical support specialists* and *help-desk technicians*. These troubleshooters interpret problems and provide technical support for hardware, software, and systems. *Network* or *computer systems administrators* design, install, and support an organization's LAN, WAN, network segment, Internet, or intranet system. They provide day-to-day on-site administrative support for software users in a variety of work environments.

Drafters

Drafters prepare technical drawings used by production workers to build everything from manufactured products, such as toys, toasters, industrial machinery, or spacecraft, to structures, such as houses, office buildings, or oil and gas pipelines. Today, many drafters use computer-aided design (CAD) systems. They sit at computer workstations and draw on a video screen. Drafters often specialize in architectural, aeronautical, electrical, electronic, civil, or mechanical work.

Engineering Technicians

Engineering technicians use the principles and theories of science, engineering, and mathematics to solve problems in research and development, manufacturing, sales, construction, and customer service. Their work is more limited in scope and more practically oriented than that of scientists and engineers. Many engineering technicians assist engineers and scientists, especially in research and development.

Library Technicians

Library technicians help librarians acquire, prepare, and organize material and assist users in finding information. Library technicians usually work under the supervision of a librarian, although they work independently in certain situations. Technicians in small libraries handle a range of duties; those in large libraries usually specialize. As libraries increasingly use new technologies—such as CD-ROM, the Internet, virtual libraries, and automated databases—the duties of library technicians will expand and evolve accordingly.

Paralegals and Legal Assistants

While lawyers assume ultimate responsibility for legal work, they often delegate many of their tasks to paralegals. In fact, paralegals—also called *legal assistants*—continue to assume a growing range of tasks in the nation's legal offices and perform many of the same tasks as lawyers. Nevertheless, they are still explicitly prohibited from carrying out duties that are considered to be the practice of law, such as setting legal fees, giving legal advice, and presenting cases in court.

Science Technicians

Science technicians use the principles and theories of science and mathematics to solve problems in research and development and to help invent and improve products and processes. However, their jobs are more practically oriented than those of scientists. Technicians set up, operate, and maintain laboratory instruments, monitor experiments, make observations, calculate and record results, and often develop conclusions. They must keep detailed logs of all their work-related activities.

Surveying and Mapping Technicians

A survey party gathers the information needed by a land surveyor. A typical survey party consists of a party chief and one or more surveying technicians and helpers. *Surveying technicians* assist land surveyors by operating survey instruments and collecting information in the field and by performing computations and computer-aided drafting in offices. *Mapping technicians* calculate mapmaking information from field notes. They also draw topographical maps and verify their accuracy.

Human Services

Occupations included in this division are primarily people-oriented. A concern for people and a desire to help them are important for anyone considering a career in Human Services. Caring about people and wanting to help them are not enough, however. Workers in this field must be skilled at leading and influencing people through teaching, counseling, ministering, providing information, and supplying other forms of assistance.

Some human services workers conduct research on various aspects of human society. Like other scientists, social scientists seek to establish facts and theories that contribute to human knowledge. Through their studies and analyses, social scientists address broad social, economic, and political questions. The Human Services cluster includes occupations organized into two groups.

SOCIAL SERVICES AND SOCIAL SCIENCES

Occupations belonging to this group are concerned with the social needs of people. Workers may deal with one person at a time or with groups of people. Social services workers usually specialize in problems that are personal, social, emotional, religious, or legal in nature.

Some workers in this group conduct basic and applied research in the social sciences. They gather, study, and analyze information about individuals, specific groups, or entire societies. Social scientists investigate all aspects of human behavior, both current and historical. These include abnormal behavior, language, work, politics, lifestyle, and cultural expression. The following occupations are included in the Social Services and Social Sciences group.

Clergy

Clergy are religious leaders, spiritual leaders, and teachers and interpreters of their traditions and faith. Most members of the clergy serve in a pulpit. They organize and lead regular religious services and officiate at special ceremonies, including confirmations, weddings, and funerals. They may lead worshipers in prayer, deliver sermons, and read from sacred texts such as the Bible, Torah, or Koran. When not conducting worship services, clergy organize, supervise, and lead religious education programs for their congregations. Clergy visit the sick or bereaved to provide comfort. They also counsel persons who are seeking religious or moral guidance.

Economists and Market and Survey Researchers

Economists study how society distributes scarce resources such as land, labor, raw materials, and machinery to produce goods and services. They conduct research, collect and analyze data, monitor economic trends, and develop forecasts. *Market research analysts* are concerned with the potential sales of a product or service. They analyze statistical data on past sales to predict future sales. *Survey researchers* design and conduct surveys.

Judges, Magistrates, and Other Judicial Workers

Judges, magistrates, and other judicial workers apply the law and oversee the legal process in courts according to local, state, and federal statutes. They preside over cases concerning every aspect of society. Traffic offenses, disputes over management of professional sports, the rights of huge corporations, and questions of disconnecting life support equipment for terminally ill persons are just a few of the issues that may be brought to a court. All judicial workers must ensure that trials and hearings are conducted fairly and that the court administers justice in a manner that safeguards the legal rights of all parties involved.

Lawyers

Lawyers, also called *attorneys*, act as both advocates and advisors in our society. As advocates, they represent one of the parties in criminal and civil trials by presenting evidence and arguing in court to support their client. As advisors, lawyers counsel their clients concerning their legal rights and obligations and suggest particular courses of action in business and personal matters.

Probation Officers and Correctional Treatment Specialists

Probation officers supervise offenders on probation or parole through personal contact with the offender and his or her family. They also attend court hearings to update the court on the offender's compliance with the terms of his or her sentence and on the offender's efforts at rehabilitation. *Correctional treatment specialists* work in correctional institutions (jails and prisons) or in parole or probation agencies. In jails and prisons, they evaluate the progress of inmates. They also work with inmates, probation officers, and other agencies to develop parole and release plans.

Psychologists

Psychologists study human behavior and mental processes to understand, explain, and change people's behavior. Some *research psychologists* investigate the physical, cognitive, emotional, or social aspects of human behavior. Other psychologists in applied fields counsel and conduct training programs; do market research; or provide mental health services in hospitals, clinics, or private settings. *Clinical psychologists*, who provide most personal counseling, constitute the largest specialty.

Recreation and Fitness Workers

People spend much of their leisure time participating in a wide variety of organized recreational activities, such as aerobics, arts and crafts, the performing arts, camping, and sports. Recreation and fitness workers plan, organize, and direct these activities in local playgrounds and recreation areas, parks, community centers, health clubs, fitness centers, religious organizations, camps, theme parks, and tourist attractions.

Social and Human Service Assistants

Social and human service assistant is a generic term for people with various job titles, including *human service worker*, *case management aide*, *social work assistant*, *community support worker*, *mental health aide*, *community outreach worker*, *life skill counselor*, or *gerontology aide*. They usually work under the direction of professionals from a variety of fields, such as nursing, psychiatry, psychology, rehabilitative or physical therapy, or social work.

Social Scientists

Social scientists study all aspects of human society. The major social science occupations include *anthropologists*, *archaeologists*, *geographers*, *historians*, *political scientists*, and *sociologists*. Their research provides insights that help us understand how individuals and groups make decisions, exercise power, or respond to change. Through their studies and analyses, social scientists assist educators, government officials, business leaders, and others in solving social, economic, and environmental problems.

Social Workers

Social workers help individuals, families, and groups cope with problems of every description. Mostly, however, they aid people who are having difficulties dealing with circumstances in their lives. These include the homeless, the unemployed, the seriously ill, the bereaved, and those with disabilities. Social workers help clients identify their concerns, consider effective solutions, and find reliable resources.

Urban and Regional Planners

Urban and regional planners, often called *community* or *city planners*, develop programs to provide for growth and revitalization of urban, suburban, and rural communities and their regions. Planners help local officials make decisions on social, economic, and environmental problems. They address such issues as central city redevelopment, traffic congestion, and the impact of growth and change on an area.

EDUCATION AND INFORMATION SERVICES

This group includes occupations in teaching, counseling, and librarianship. Teachers help students gain the knowledge and skills needed to function in the world. Counselors provide personal, social, and career guidance in a wide range of settings. Librarians manage libraries and learning centers. They assist individuals with information needs ranging from recreational reading to specialized research. Archivists and curators also help people learn and gain information, but they work primarily with objects such as historical documents. The following occupations are included in the Education and Information Services group.

Archivists and Curators

Archivists and curators search for, acquire, analyze, describe, catalog, restore, preserve, exhibit, maintain, and store items of lasting value. They plan and oversee the work of maintaining collections. These collections may consist of historical documents, audiovisual materials, corporate records, art, coins, stamps, minerals, clothing, maps, or historic sites.

Counselors

Counselors help people evaluate their interests and abilities. They advise people and assist them with personal, social, educational, and career problems and concerns. The duties of counselors depend on the individuals they serve and the settings in which they work. Common titles include *educational and school counselor*, *vocational or employment counselor*, *rehabilitation counselor*, and *mental health counselor*.

Instructional Coordinators

Instructional coordinators, also known as *curriculum specialists*, *staff development specialists* or *directors of instructional material*, play a large role in improving the quality of education in the classroom. They develop instructional materials, train teachers, and assess educational programs in terms of quality and adherence to regulations and standards. They also assist in implementing new technology in the classroom. Instructional coordinators often specialize in specific subjects, such as language arts, mathematics, or social studies.

Librarians

Librarians assist people in finding information and using it effectively for personal and professional purposes. They collect, organize, and lend books, periodicals, videotapes, DVDs, CD-ROMs, audiocassettes, and other types of materials to different users. Librarians are classified according to the type of library in which they work: public libraries, school library/media centers, academic libraries, and special libraries. The most familiar type of library is the public library.

Teacher Assistants

Teacher assistants provide instructional and clerical support for classroom teachers, allowing teachers more time for lesson planning and teaching. Teacher assistants tutor and assist children in learning class material using the teacher's lesson plans, providing students with individualized attention. Teacher assistants also supervise students in the cafeteria, schoolyard, or school discipline center or on field trips. They record grades, set up equipment, and help prepare materials for instruction. Teacher assistants are also called *teacher aides* or *instructional aides*.

Teachers—Adult Literacy and Remedial and Self-Enrichment Education

Adult literacy and remedial education teachers provide adults and out-of-school youths with the education needed to read, write, and speak English and to perform basic math calculations. Adult literacy and remedial education classes are made up of students who dropped out of school or who passed through the school system without receiving an adequate education. *Self-enrichment teachers* teach courses that students take for personal enrichment, in areas such as cooking, dancing, creative writing, photography, or personal finance.

Teachers—Postsecondary

Education beyond high school is called postsecondary education. *College and university faculty*, who make up the majority of postsecondary teachers, teach and advise two- and four-year college and university students and perform a significant part of the nation's research. *Postsecondary career and technical education teachers* provide instruction for occupations that do not require a college degree, such as dental hygienist, x-ray technician, auto mechanic, and cosmetologist. Classes often are taught in a setting in which students are provided with hands-on experience.

Teachers—Preschool, Kindergarten, Elementary, Middle, and Secondary

Preschool, kindergarten, elementary, and *middle school teachers* play a vital role in the development of young children. They introduce children to numbers, language, science, and social studies. *Secondary school teachers* provide more advanced instruction into subjects introduced in earlier grades. Secondary school teachers specialize in specific subjects, such as English, Spanish, mathematics, biology, business education, history, physical education, or biology. All teachers spend considerable time in planning, implementing, and evaluating instruction.

Teachers—Special Education

Special education teachers work with children and youths who have a variety of disabilities. However, the majority of special education teachers work with children with mild to moderate disabilities, using the general education curriculum, or modifying it to meet the child's individual needs. Most special education teachers instruct students at the elementary, middle, and secondary school level, although some teachers work with infants and toddlers.

Personal and Public Services

Workers in service occupations perform a wide variety of tasks for individuals and the general public. The largest group of service workers is in the food service occupations. These are the workers who prepare and serve food and beverages. Another large group of workers provides personal services to individuals. These services may include cutting and styling hair, caring for children and elderly persons, and cleaning and caring for houses and lawns. Services such as these make life easier and more pleasant for people. An interest in providing services for the convenience of others is required for personal service occupations.

The smallest, and perhaps the most important, group of service workers are the police officers, firefighters, guards, and others who safeguard our lives and property. An interest in enforcing laws and using authority to protect people and property is important for protective service workers.

Most of the occupations in this cluster require no previous training or short-term and on-the-job training. Service occupations require the ability to deal effectively with people. It is important for service workers to pay close attention to their customers. Dissatisfied customers are not likely to return. A pleasant, outgoing personality helps a great deal in jobs that involve pleasing a paying customer. The following occupations are included in the Personal and Public Services cluster.

Animal Care and Service Workers

Many people like animals. But, as pet owners can attest, taking care of them is hard work. Animal care and service workers, who include *animal caretakers* and *animal trainers*, train, feed, water, groom, bathe, and exercise animals and clean, disinfect, and repair their cages. They also play with the animals, provide companionship, and observe behavioral changes that could indicate illness or injury. Boarding kennels, animal shelters, veterinary hospitals and clinics, stables, laboratories, aquariums, and zoological parks all house animals and employ animal care and service workers.

Barbers, Cosmetologists, and Other Personal Appearance Workers

Barbers and cosmetologists, also called *hairdressers* and *hairstylists*, help people look neat and well groomed. Other personal appearance workers, such as *manicurists and pedicurists*, *shampooers*, and *skin care specialists*, provide specialized services that help clients look and feel their best. Barbers, cosmetologists, and other personal appearance workers who operate their own salons have managerial duties that include hiring, supervising, and firing workers, as well as keeping business and inventory records, ordering supplies, and arranging for advertising.

Building Cleaning Workers

Building cleaning workers, including *janitors*, *executive housekeepers*, *maids*, and *housekeeping cleaners*, keep office buildings, hospitals, stores, apartment houses, hotels, and other types of buildings clean and in good condition. Some only do cleaning, while others have a wide range of duties. Cleaning supervisors coordinate, schedule, and supervise the activities of janitors and cleaners.

Chefs, Cooks, and Food Preparation Workers

A reputation for serving good food is essential to the success of any restaurant or hotel, whether it offers sandwiches or exotic cuisine. *Chefs, cooks, and food preparation workers* are largely responsible for establishing and maintaining this reputation. Chefs and cooks do this by preparing meals, while other food preparation workers assist them by cleaning surfaces, peeling vegetables, and performing other duties.

Child-care Workers

Child-care workers nurture and teach children of all ages in child-care centers, nursery schools, preschools, public schools, private households, family child-care homes, and before- and after-school programs. These workers play an important role in a child's development by caring for the child when parents are at work or away for other reasons. In addition to attending to children's basic needs, these workers organize activities that stimulate the children's physical, emotional, intellectual, and social growth.

Correctional Officers

Correctional officers are responsible for overseeing individuals who have been arrested and are awaiting trial or who have been convicted of a crime and sentenced to serve time in a jail, reformatory, or penitentiary. They maintain security and inmate accountability to prevent disturbances, assaults, or escapes. Correctional officers have no law enforcement responsibilities outside the institution where they work.

Firefighting Occupations

Firefighters help protect the public against losses causes by fire. Firefighters must be prepared to respond to a fire and handle any emergency that arises. At a fire, firefighters perform specific duties as assigned by an officer. They may connect hose lines to hydrants, operate a pump, or position ladders. They may rescue victims, administer emergency medical aid, ventilate smoke-filled areas, and salvage the contents of buildings. Most fire departments also are responsible for fire prevention.

Flight Attendants

Flight attendants are aboard almost all passenger planes to look after the passengers' flight safety and comfort. As passengers board the plane, attendants greet them, check their tickets, and assist them in storing coats and carry-on luggage. Prior to takeoff, attendants instruct passengers in the use of emergency equipment and check to see that seat belts are fastened. In the air, they answer questions about the flight, distribute magazines, pillows, and other items, and respond to passenger requests. After the plane has landed, flight attendants assist passengers as they leave the plane.

Food and Beverage Serving and Related Occupations

Whether they work in small, informal diners or large, elegant restaurants, all food and beverage serving and related workers strive to help customers have a positive dining experience in their establishments. The largest group of these workers, *waiters and waitresses*, take customers' orders, serve food and beverages, prepare itemized checks, and sometimes accept payments. *Bartenders* fill drink orders that waiters and waitresses take from customers. *Hosts and hostesses* try to create a good impression of a restaurant by warmly welcoming guests. *Dining room and cafeteria attendants and bartender helpers* assist waiters, waitresses, and bartenders by cleaning tables, removing dirty dishes, and keeping serving areas stocked with supplies.

Gaming Services Occupations

Legalized gambling in the United States today includes casino gaming, state lotteries, pari-mutuel wagering on contests such as horse racing, and charitable gaming. Gaming, the playing of games of chance, is a multibillion-dollar industry that is responsible for the creation of a number of unique service occupations. The majority of all gaming services workers are employed in casinos. Their duties and titles may vary from one establishment to another.

Grounds Maintenance Workers

Attractively designed, healthy, and well-maintained lawns, gardens, and grounds create a positive first impression, establish a peaceful mood, and increase property values. Grounds maintenance workers—sometimes called *gardeners* or *groundskeepers*—perform the variety of tasks necessary to achieve a pleasant and functional outdoor environment. They also care for indoor gardens and plantings in commercial and public facilities, such as malls, hotels, and botanical gardens.

Personal and Home Care Aides

Personal and home care aides help the elderly, people with disabilities, and ill persons live in their own homes or in residential care facilities instead of in a health facility. Most work with elderly clients or clients with disabilities who need more extensive care than family or friends can provide. Some aides work with families in which a parent is incapacitated and small children need care. Others help discharged hospital patients who have relatively short-term needs.

Pest Control Workers

Pest control workers, most of whom work for pest control companies, locate, identify, destroy, and repel pests. They use their knowledge of pests' lifestyles and habits, along with an arsenal of pest management techniques—applying chemicals, setting traps, operating equipment, and even modifying structures—to alleviate pest problems.

Police and Detectives

People depend on police officers and detectives to protect their lives and property. Law enforcement officers perform these duties in a variety of ways, depending on the size and type of their organization. In most jurisdictions, they are expected to exercise authority when necessary, whether on or off duty. About 65 percent of state and local law enforcement officers are uniformed personnel, including *police*, *detectives*, *sheriffs and deputies*, and *state police officers*.

Private Detectives and Investigators

Private detectives and investigators use many means to determine the facts in a variety of matters. To carry out investigations, they may use various types of surveillance or searches. To verify facts, they may make phone calls or visit a subject's workplace. In other cases, especially those involving missing persons and background checks, investigators often interview people to gather as much information as possible about an individual. In all cases, private detectives and investigators assist attorneys, businesses, and the public with a variety of legal, financial, and personal problems.

Security Guards and Gaming Surveillance Officers

Guards, also called *security officers*, patrol and inspect property to protect against fire, theft, vandalism, and illegal entry. Common employers include banks, hospitals, shopping malls, airports, government buildings, museums, factories, and nightclubs. Some guards work at specific gatherings such as concerts, conventions, sporting events, or similar affairs. Guards usually are uniformed and may carry a nightstick and gun. *Gaming surveillance officers and gaming investigators* act as security agents for casino managers and patrons.

Health Services

Caring for the sick is one of the world's oldest occupations. People have been doing it for thousands of years. But ways of taking care of the sick have changed a great deal. Centuries ago, health care was often based on magic, superstition, and ignorance. For example, operations took place in unsanitary surroundings because doctors did not realize that germs caused infections. Today, medicine is based on science and research.

Our current knowledge of health and medicine is the result of centuries of scientific observation and research. New medical discoveries and advances are being made all the time. Many current Health Services occupations are the result of new developments in medicine and technology. It seems likely that future discoveries and new technology will exert a strong influence on this field, as they have in the past.

Medical practitioners, such as physicians, are among the most highly trained and highly skilled workers in our economy. The largest numbers of health services workers, however, are those involved in technical-level health occupations. Health Services is a large and growing cluster of occupations, combining an interest in science with an interest in preventing, diagnosing, and treating diseases, disorders, and injuries. The Health Services cluster includes occupations organized into three groups.

HEALTH DIAGNOSING PRACTITIONERS

Health practitioners diagnose, treat, and strive to prevent illness and disease. While all of them practice the art of healing, they differ in methods of treatment and areas of specialization. Physicians prescribe medications, exercise, proper diet, and surgery, which surgeons perform. Manipulation of muscles and bones, especially the spine, is the primary form of treatment given by chiropractors. Optometrists specialize in eye care, and podiatrists treat foot diseases and deformities. Dentists emphasize both the treatment and the prevention of problems associated with teeth and gums. Veterinarians treat animals.

Training to become a health practitioner is much more rigorous than training for most other occupations. But the practice of medicine offers the potential for high income and great prestige within the community. Most health practitioners derive satisfaction from knowing that their work contributes directly to the well-being of others.

All health practitioners must have the ability and perseverance to complete the years of study required. They should be emotionally stable, be able to make decisions in emergencies, and have a strong desire to help the sick and injured. Sincerity and an ability to gain the confidence of patients also are important qualities. The following occupations are included in the Health Diagnosing Practitioners group.

Chiropractors

Chiropractors, also known as *doctors of chiropractic* or *chiropractic physicians*, diagnose and treat patients whose health problems are associated with the body's muscular, nervous, and skeletal systems, especially the spine. Chiropractors believe that misalignment of spinal vertebrae or irritation of the spinal nerves can affect the nervous system. This in turn can alter many important bodily functions. Chiropractors stress the patient's overall well-being. They encourage the use of natural, nonsurgical health treatments that do not involve the use of drugs.

Dentists

Dentists diagnose and treat problems of the teeth and tissues of the mouth. They take x-rays, place protective sealants on teeth, fill cavities, straighten teeth, repair fractured teeth, and treat gum disease. Dentists remove teeth and make molds and measurements for dentures to replace missing teeth. They also perform corrective surgery of the gums and supporting bones. Increasingly, dentists are concerned with preventing dental problems.

Optometrists

Optometrists are primary eye-care providers who examine people's eyes to diagnose and treat vision problems and, in some cases, eye disease. They also test to ensure that the patient has proper depth and color perception and the ability to focus and coordinate the eyes. They analyze test results and develop a treatment plan. Optometrists prescribe eyeglasses, contact lenses, vision therapy, and low-vision aids.

Physicians and Surgeons

Physicians are medical doctors who perform medical examinations, diagnose illnesses, and treat people suffering from injury or disease. They advise patients on diet, hygiene, and preventative health care. They use all accepted methods of treatment, including drugs and surgery. Most MDs specialize in a particular area of medicine such as internal medicine, dermatology, or pediatrics. *Surgeons* are physicians who specialize in the treatment of injury, disease, and deformity through operations.

Podiatrists

The human foot is a complex structure. It contains twenty-six bones, plus muscles, nerves, ligaments, and blood vessels, all designed for balance and mobility. Podiatrists, also known as *doctors of podiatric medicine* (DPMs), diagnose and treat disorders and diseases of the foot and lower leg. In treating these problems, podiatrists prescribe drugs, order physical therapy, and perform surgery. They also fit corrective inserts called *orthotics* and design custom-made shoes.

Veterinarians

Veterinarians care for pets, livestock, and sporting and laboratory animals. They also protect humans against diseases carried by animals. They diagnose medical problems, dress wounds, set broken bones, perform surgery, prescribe and administer medicines, and vaccinate animals against diseases. They advise owners on care and breeding. The majority treat small companion animals such as dogs, cats, and birds.

HEALTH ASSESSMENT AND TREATING OCCUPATIONS

Health services workers described in this section care for the sick, help the disabled, and advise individuals and communities on ways of maintaining and improving their health. Nursing is by far the largest of these occupations.

Registered nurses work primarily in hospitals, where they provide patient care, assist in surgery and diagnostic procedures, train and supervise staff, handle administrative tasks, and perform other duties. The relatively new occupation of physician assistant involves direct patient care by workers who are trained to perform many tasks normally done by a physician. Therapists use a variety of techniques to help patients who are injured, physically or mentally disabled, or emotionally disturbed. Dietitians and pharmacists also use special skills and expertise to assist sick or disabled persons, although they do not provide direct patient care.

Most occupations in this group require a college degree. Some require a license to practice. An interest in caring for and treating patients is required for these occupations. The following occupations are included in the Health Assessment and Treating Occupations group.

Dietitians and Nutritionists

Dietitians and nutritionists plan nutrition programs and supervise the preparation and serving of meals. They help prevent and treat illnesses by promoting healthful eating habits. They scientifically evaluate a client's diet and suggest modifications. Dietitians also counsel groups and set up and supervise food service systems for institutions such as hospitals, prisons, and schools.

Occupational Therapists

Occupational therapists help individuals with mental, physical, developmental, or emotional disabilities to develop, recover, or maintain daily living and work skills. They help patients improve basic motor functions and reasoning abilities, as well as learn to dress, bathe, cook, or operate machinery. Occupational therapists also assist patients with permanent disabilities in coping with the physical and emotional effects of the disabilities.

Pharmacists

Pharmacists measure, count, mix, and dispense drugs and medicines prescribed by physicians, podiatrists and dentists. They advise the public on the proper selection and use of medicines. They also advise physicians and other health professionals on the selection, dosage, and effect of medications. Most pharmacists create and maintain computerized records of patients' medical profiles and drug therapies.

Physical Therapists

Physical therapists improve the mobility, relieve the pain, and prevent or limit the permanent disability of patients suffering from injuries or disease. Their patients include accident victims and individuals with disabilities resulting from such conditions as multiple sclerosis, cerebral palsy, nerve injuries, amputations, head injuries, fractures, low back pain, arthritis, and heart disease.

Physician Assistants

As their title suggests, physician assistants (PAs) support physicians. They are trained to perform many of the routine but time-consuming tasks physicians usually do. They take medical histories, perform physical examinations, order laboratory tests and x-rays, make preliminary diagnoses, and give inoculations. They also treat minor injuries. Physician assistants always work under the supervision of a physician.

Recreational Therapists

Recreational therapists employ medically approved activities to improve or maintain the mental, physical, and emotional well-being of patients. Activities include sports, games, dance, drama, arts and crafts, music, and field trips. They help individuals recover basic motor functioning and reasoning abilities, build confidence, and socialize effectively to enable them to be more independent, as well as to reduce or eliminate the effects of illness or disability.

Registered Nurses

Registered nurses (RNs) care for the sick and injured and help people stay well. They observe, assess, and record symptoms, reactions, and progress; assist physicians during treatments and examinations; administer medications; assist in convalescence and rehabilitation; instruct patients and their families in proper care; and help individuals and groups take steps to improve or maintain their health. State laws govern the tasks RNs may perform.

Respiratory Therapists

Respiratory therapists evaluate, treat, and care for patients with breathing disorders. In diagnosis, therapists test the capacity of the lungs. Treatment may range from giving temporary relief to patients with chronic asthma or emphysema to emergency care for heart failure, stroke, drowning, or shock. The most common treatments are oxygen or oxygen mixtures, chest physiotherapy, and aerosol medications.

Speech/Language Pathologists and Audiologists

Speech/language pathologists identify and treat speech, language, and swallowing disorders resulting from conditions such as hearing loss, brain injury, cerebral palsy, cleft palate, voice pathology, mental retardation, faulty learning, emotional problems, or foreign dialect. They use a variety of treatment tools, including audiovisual equipment and computers. *Audiologists* identify, assess, treat, and work to prevent hearing problems.

HEALTH TECHNOLOGISTS, TECHNICIANS, ASSISTANTS, AND AIDES

Many occupations in the health services field owe their existence to the development of new laboratory procedures, diagnostic techniques, and treatment methods. Quite a few of these involve clinical applications of the computer. Clinical laboratories have been transformed by the installation of automated instruments that offer low-cost analyses in minutes. Elsewhere in the hospital, new kinds of equipment have made possible earlier and more accurate diagnoses and more effective treatment. Many of the occupations in this section involve operating or monitoring biomedical equipment.

Most occupations in this group are designed to extend the services of highly skilled health practitioners. For example, dental hygienists expand dental services without sacrificing the quality of care. Emergency medical technicians are specially trained to provide medical attention when no physician or nurse is available. Surgical technicians assist before, during, and after surgery.

The distinction between a health technologist and a health technician lies in the complexity of the job. Technologists have more responsibility than technicians and therefore need more training.

Technicians generally have more responsibility and training than assistants and aides. The biggest difference, however, between assistants and aides and other workers in this group is the type of work they do. Health service assistants and aides help provide services to individuals. They typically perform routine but essential tasks that involve a great deal of personal contact. This may include conversing with patients, making them comfortable, and setting them at ease. They might also make appointments, greet patients, keep records, set up equipment, deliver food trays, and help patients with exercises.

Occupations in this group generally require training beyond high school, but less than a college degree. Most call for one or two years of formal education or training. For many of the occupations in this group, an interest in using medical equipment or performing medical procedures is required. The following occupations are included in the Health Technologists, Technicians, Assistants, and Aides group.

Cardiovascular Technologists and Technicians

Cardiovascular technologists and technicians assist physicians in diagnosing and treating heart (cardiac) and blood vessel (vascular) ailments. One type of technician, called an *EKG technician,* operates a machine called an electrocardiograph to trace electrical impulses transmitted by the heart. *Cardiology technologists* assist physicians with a specialized procedure in which a small tube, or catheter, is inserted into a patient's blood vessel from a spot on the leg. This is done to determine if a blockage exists and for other diagnostic purposes and procedures.

Clinical Laboratory Technologists and Technicians

Laboratory testing plays a crucial role in the detection, diagnosis, and treatment of disease. Clinical (medical) laboratory technologists and technicians perform most of these tests. *Medical technologists* perform complex chemical, biological, hematological, immunologic, microscopic, and bacteriological tests. *Medical laboratory technicians* perform routine tests and laboratory procedures. Like technologists, they may work in several different areas of the clinical laboratory or specialize in just one.

Dental Assistants

Dental assistants perform a variety of patient care, office, and laboratory duties. They work at chair-side as dentists examine and treat patients. Assistants hand dentists the proper instruments and materials and keep patients' mouths dry and clear by using suction or other devices. Some dental assistants prepare materials for making impressions and restorations, expose radiographs, and process dental x-ray film as directed by a dentist.

Dental Hygienists

Who cleans your teeth? It is probably a dental hygienist. Dental hygienists evaluate a patient's teeth and mouth and record their findings. They remove tartar, stains, and plaque from above and below the gum line; apply cavity-preventive agents; and expose and develop dental x-rays. In some states, dental hygienists place temporary fillings and dressings; remove sutures; and smooth and polish metal restorations (fillings, crowns, and the like). Dental hygienists also help patients develop and maintain good oral health.

Diagnostic Medical Sonographers

Diagnostic medical sonographers, also known as *ultrasonographers*, use special equipment to direct high-frequency sound waves into areas of a patient's body. Sonographers operate the equipment, which collects reflected echoes and forms an image that may be videotaped, transmitted, or photographed for interpretation and diagnosis by a physician.

Emergency Medical Technicians and Paramedics

People's lives often depend on the quick reaction and competent care of *emergency medical technicians* (EMTs) and *paramedics*, who are EMTs with additional advanced training to perform more difficult medical procedures. Incidents as varied as automobile accidents, heart attacks, drowning, childbirth, and gunshot wounds all require immediate medical attention. EMTs and paramedics provide this vital attention as they care for the sick or injured and transport them to a medical facility.

Licensed Practical and Licensed Vocational Nurses

Licensed practical nurses (LPNs), or *licensed vocational nurses* (LVNs) as they are called in Texas and California, care for people who are sick, injured, or convalescing or who have disabilities under the direction of physicians and registered nurses. They take such vital signs as temperature, blood pressure, pulse, and respiration. They treat bedsores, prepare and give injections and enemas, apply dressings, give alcohol rubs and massages, and insert catheters. They also help patients with bathing, dressing, and personal hygiene; feed them and record food and liquid intake and output; keep them comfortable; and care for their emotional needs.

Medical Assistants

Medical assistants perform routine administrative and clinical tasks to keep the offices and clinics of physicians, podiatrists, chiropractors, and optometrists running smoothly. Duties vary from office to office and from state to state. In small practices, medical assistants are usually generalists, handling both administrative and clinical duties. They report directly to the office manager, physician, or other health practitioner. Those in large practices tend to specialize in a particular area under the supervision of department administrators. In some states, tasks may include helping physicians examine and treat patients.

Medical Records and Health Information Technicians

Doctors and hospitals set up a permanent file for every patient they treat. This file is known as the medical record, or chart. It includes the patient's medical history, results of physical examinations, reports of x-ray and laboratory tests, diagnoses, treatment plans, and notes by doctors, nurses, and other medical personnel. Medical records and health information technicians organize these records and evaluate them for completeness and accuracy.

Medical Transcriptionists

Medical transcriptionists, also called *medical transcribers* and *medical stenographers*, listen to dictated recordings made by physicians and other health care professionals and transcribe them into medical reports, correspondence, and other administrative material. These documents eventually become part of patients' permanent files.

Nuclear Medicine Technologists

Nuclear medicine is the branch of radiology that used radionuclides (unstable atoms that emit radiation spontaneously) to diagnose and treat disease. Radionuclides are purified and compounded like other drugs to form radiopharmaceuticals. These radiopharmaceuticals may be injected into a patient or taken orally. The radioactivity can then be detected and monitored from outside the body to assess the characteristics or functioning of those tissues or organs in which it settles. Nuclear medicine technologists perform these radioactive tests and procedures under the supervision of physicians.

Nursing, Psychiatric, and Home Health Aides

Nursing and psychiatric aides help care for physically or mentally ill, injured, disabled, or infirm individuals confined to hospitals, nursing and personal care facilities, and mental health settings. The duties of home health aides are similar, but they work in patients' homes or residential care facilities. *Nursing aides*, also known as *nursing assistants, geriatric aides, unlicensed assistive personnel*, or *hospital attendants*, perform routine tasks under the supervision of nursing and medical staff. *Psychiatric aides*, also known as *mental health assistants* or *psychiatric nursing assistants*, care for mentally impaired or emotionally disturbed individuals. *Home health aides* help elderly, convalescent, or disabled persons live in their own homes instead of in a health facility.

Occupational Health and Safety Specialists and Technicians

Occupational health and safety specialists and technicians, also known as *occupational health and safety inspectors* and *industrial hygienists*, help keep workplaces safe. They promote occupational health and safety within organizations by developing safer, healthier, and more efficient ways of working. *Occupational health and safety specialists* analyze work environments and design programs to control, eliminate, and prevent disease or injury caused by chemical, physical, and biological agents or ergonomic factors. *Occupational health and safety technicians* collect data on work environments for analysis by occupational health and safety specialists.

Occupational Therapist Assistants and Aides

Occupational therapist assistants and aides work under the direction of occupational therapists to provide rehabilitative services to persons with mental, physical, emotional, or developmental impairments. *Occupational therapist assistants* help clients with rehabilitative activities and exercises outlined in a treatment plan developed in collaboration with an occupational therapist. *Occupational therapist aides* typically prepare materials and assemble equipment used during treatment. They are also responsible for a range of clerical tasks.

Opticians, Dispensing

After an eye exam by an ophthalmologist or an optometrist, a prescription for corrective lenses may be written. Dispensing opticians fill such prescriptions by fitting eyeglasses or contact lenses. Dispensing opticians help customers select appropriate frames, order the necessary ophthalmic laboratory work, and adjust the finished eyeglasses. In some states, they fit contact lenses under the supervision of an optometrist or ophthalmologist.

Pharmacy Aides

Pharmacy aides help licensed pharmacists with administrative duties in running a pharmacy. Aides often are clerks or cashiers who primarily answer telephones, handle money, stock shelves, and perform other clerical duties. They work closely with pharmacy technicians. Pharmacy technicians usually perform more complex tasks than do assistants, although in some states, their duties and job titles overlap.

Pharmacy Technicians

Pharmacy technicians help licensed pharmacists provide medication and other health care products to patients. Technicians usually perform routine tasks to help prepare prescribed medication for patients, such as counting tablets and labeling bottles. Technicians refer any questions regarding prescriptions, drug information, or health matters to a pharmacist.

Physical Therapist Assistants and Aides

Physical therapist assistants and aides perform components of physical therapy procedures and related tasks selected by a supervising physical therapist. *Physical therapist assistants* perform a variety of tasks involving exercises, massages, electrical stimulation, paraffin baths, hot and cold packs, traction, and ultrasound. *Physical therapist aides* help make therapy sessions productive, under the direct supervision of a physical therapist or physical therapist assistant. They are usually responsible for keeping the treatment area clean and organized and preparing for each patient's therapy.

Radiologic Technologists and Technicians

Radiologic technologists and technicians take x-rays and administer nonradioactive materials into patients' bloodstreams for diagnostic purposes. Some specialize in diagnostic imaging technologies such as computed tomography (CT) and magnetic resonance imaging (MRI). *Radiologic technologists and technicians*, also referred to as *radiographers*, produce x-ray films (radiographs) of parts of the human body for use in diagnosing medical problems. Some radiographers, called *CT technologists*, operate CT scanners to produce cross-sectional images of patients. Others operate machines using strong magnets and radio waves rather than radiation to create an image and are called *magnetic resonance imaging (MRI) technologists*.

Surgical Technologists

Surgical technologists, also called *scrubs* and *surgical or operating room technicians,* assist in operations under the supervision of surgeons, registered nurses, or other surgical personnel. They help set up the operating room with surgical instruments, equipment, sterile (germ-free) linens, and sterile solutions. Surgical technologists also prepare patients for surgery. They transport patients to the operating room, help position them on the operating table, and cover them with sterile surgical cloths, or drapes.

Arts, Communications, and Entertainment

Workers in the performing arts, the visual arts, communications, and entertainment use a variety of media and venues to express ideas and emotions. For people with creativity, imagination, and talent, these occupations offer unmatched opportunities for self-expression.

The performing arts include the areas of instrumental music, singing, acting, and dance. All have in common the goal of communicating with and influencing the emotions of the audience. Through the media of music, speech, and movement, performing artists may communicate a message or simply provide entertainment. In addition to the performing arts, athletic and sporting events provide entertainment and enjoyment to millions of viewers.

The visual arts include design, fine and applied arts, and photography. These occupations use visual means such as light, space, color, and texture to convey feelings or create a particular result. The artistic product might be created primarily to express an emotion or feeling. Or the creative product might serve a practical purpose.

Imagine the world without television, films, newspapers, magazines, or books.

Communications includes occupations having to do with research, writing, editing, and production. Communication is a process that begins with observing what is happening and analyzing and interpreting that information. The information is then transmitted to an audience through a variety of media. People in communications occupations use the written or spoken word to inform, persuade, or entertain others.

Arts, communications, and entertainment occupations require varying levels of education and training. For many occupations in this group, creativity, talent, and athletic ability are more important than educational preparation. People who aspire to a career in arts, communications, and entertainment need to be realistic about their talent. Competition for these types of jobs is keen. Practical experience—in a local theatrical production or on a community newspaper, for example—can help in getting started. Even very talented people must be willing to spend years mastering a skill and then waiting for a break to perform, to exhibit their work, or to have a manuscript published. The following occupations are included in the Arts, Communications, and Entertainment cluster.

Actors, Producers, and Directors

Actors entertain and communicate with people through dramatic roles. They rely on facial and verbal expressions as well as body motion to create a certain effect. Making a character come to life before an audience is a rewarding job. *Producers* select plays or scripts and hire directors, key cast members, and production staff. Producers coordinate the activities of writers, directors, managers, and other personnel. *Directors* interpret plays or scripts. They select cast members as well as direct the work of the cast and crew.

Announcers

Announcers in radio and television perform a variety of tasks on and off the air. They announce station program information such as program schedules and station breaks for commercials or public service information, and they introduce and close programs. Announcers read prepared scripts or provide ad-lib commentary on the air when presenting news, sports, weather, and commercials. If a written script is required, they may do the research and writing. Announcers also interview guests and moderate panels or discussions. Some provide commentary for the audience during sporting events, parades, and other events. Announcers are often well known to radio and television audiences.

Artists and Related Workers

Artists create art to communicate ideas, thoughts, or feelings. Artists generally fall into one of three categories. *Art directors* formulate design concepts and presentation approaches for visual communications media. *Fine artists*, including *painters*, *sculptors*, and *illustrators*, create original artwork using a variety of media and techniques. *Multimedia artists and animators* create special effects, animation, or other visual images using film, video, computers, or other electronic media.

Athletes, Coaches, Umpires, and Related Workers

We are a nation of sports fans and sports players. Interest in watching sports continues to grow, resulting in expanding leagues, new leagues, and more and larger venues in which to witness amateur and professional competitions. *Athletes* compete in organized, officiated sports events to entertain spectators. *Coaches* organize and instruct amateur and professional athletes in fundamentals of individual and team sports. In individual sports, *instructors* may often fill this role. *Umpires* and *referees* officiate at competitive athletic and sporting events.

Dancers and Choreographers

From ancient times to the present, *dancers* have expressed ideas, stories, rhythm, and sound with their bodies. Some dancers perform in classical ballet or modern dance. Others perform in dance adaptations for musical shows; in folk, ethnic, and jazz dances; and in other popular kinds of dancing. *Choreographers* often create original dances, teach these dances to performers, and sometimes direct and stage the presentations of their work.

Designers

Designers are people with a desire to create. They combine practical knowledge with artistic ability to turn abstract ideas into formal designs for the merchandise we buy, the clothes we wear, the publications we read, and the living and office space we inhabit. Designers usually specialize in one particular area of design; for example, automobiles, clothing, furniture, home appliances, industrial equipment, movie and theater sets, packaging, or floral arrangements. Designers sometimes supervise assistants who carry out their creations.

Musicians, Singers, and Related Workers

Musicians, singers, and related workers may play instruments, sing, write compositions, or conduct instrumental or vocal performances. *Instrumental musicians* play a musical instrument in an orchestra, band, or jazz combo. *Singers* perform character parts or sing in their individual styles. *Composers* create original music such as symphonies, operas, sonatas, or popular songs. *Conductors* lead orchestras and bands. *Choral directors* conduct choirs and glee clubs.

News Analysts, Reporters, and Correspondents

News analysts, reporters, and correspondents play a key role in our society. They gather information, prepare stories, and make broadcasts that inform us about local, state, national, and international events. *News analysts* examine, interpret, and broadcast news received from various sources. *Weathercasters* report current and forecasted weather conditions. *Sportscasters* select, write, and deliver sports news. This may include interviews with sports personalities and coverage of games and other sporting events. In covering a story, *reporters* investigate leads and news tips, look at documents, observe events at the scene, and interview people. In some cases, *news writers* write a story from information collected and submitted by reporters. *News correspondents* report on news occurring in the large U.S. and foreign cities where they are stationed.

Photographers

Photographers produce and preserve images that paint a picture, tell a story, or record an event. To create commercial-quality photographs, photographers need both technical expertise and creativity. Producing a successful picture requires choosing and presenting a subject to achieve a particular effect and selecting the appropriate equipment. Photographers use either a traditional camera or a digital camera that electronically records images.

Public Relations Specialists

The public reputation and profitability of a company can depend on how successfully it presents its goals and policies to the public. Public relations specialists handle such functions as press, community, consumer, and governmental relations; political campaigns; interest group representation;

fund-raising; and employee relations. Understanding the attitudes and concerns of the public and communicating this information to management are also important parts of the job.

Television, Video, and Motion Picture Camera Operators and Editors

Making commercial-quality movies and video programs calls for technical expertise and creativity. Producing successful images requires choosing and presenting interesting material, selecting appropriate equipment, and applying a good eye and steady hand to ensure smooth, natural movement of the camera. *Television, video, and motion picture camera operators* produce images that inform or entertain an audience or record an event. *Film and video editors* edit soundtracks, film, and video for the motion picture, cable, and broadcast television industries. Some camera operators do their own editing.

Writers and Editors

Writers and editors communicate through the written word. Writers and editors generally fall into one of three categories. *Writers and authors* develop original fiction and nonfiction for books, magazines and trade journals, newspapers, web sites, company newsletters, radio and television broadcasts, movies, and advertisements. *Technical writers* put scientific and technical information into easily understandable language. They produce scientific and technical reports, equipment manuals, operating and maintenance instructions, and the like. *Editors* select and prepare material for publication or broadcast and review and prepare a writer's work for publication or dissemination.

Business and Marketing

The downtown section of a typical American city has dozens of large office buildings housing hundreds of different businesses. Included are banks, investment companies, insurance companies, department stores, specialty retail stores, hotels, travel agencies, law firms, and many others. Businesses such as these employ large numbers of office and sales workers.

Workers in this cluster make products and services available to the consumer. They also provide a number of business and administrative support services. The Business and Marketing cluster includes occupations organized into two groups.

MARKETING AND SALES

Sales work offers a wide range of employment opportunities. In some sales jobs, people are their own bosses, set their own schedules, and have their earnings depend entirely upon their performance. Other jobs are more routine, with structured work schedules and guaranteed hourly wages. Supervisory positions in sales enable individuals to use their leadership and administrative abilities to plan, organize, and coordinate retail, wholesale, insurance, real estate, and other sales activities. In all kinds of sales work, opportunities are good for flexible or part-time working hours.

Personal attributes are more important in marketing and sales than in most other occupations. Sales workers must be outgoing, enthusiastic, and persuasive. They have to be poised and at ease with strangers, as well as good at striking up a conversation and relating to other people. Success in sales takes initiative, energy, self-confidence, and self-discipline. The following occupations are included in the Marketing and Sales group.

Cashiers

Supermarkets, department stores, movie theaters, restaurants, and many other businesses employ cashiers. Most cashiers total bills, receive money, make change, fill out charge forms, and give receipts. Although cash registers are still used, an increasing number of establishments employ scanners and computer terminals. Cashiers may also handle returns and exchanges.

Counter and Rental Clerks

Whether choosing a videotape, dropping off clothes to be dry-cleaned, or renting a car, we rely on counter and rental clerks to handle these transactions efficiently. Counter and rental clerks are responsible for answering questions, taking orders, receiving payments, and accepting returns. In addition, they may do some selling when sales workers are unavailable.

Demonstrators, Product Promoters, and Models

Demonstrators and product promoters interest the public in buying a product by demonstrating it to prospective customers and answering their questions. They may sell the demonstrated merchandise or gather names of prospects to contact at a later date or to pass on to sales staff. *Demonstrators* promote sales of a product to consumers, while *product promoters* try to induce retail stores to sell particular products and market them effectively. *Models* pose for photos or as subjects for paintings or sculptures. They display clothing, such as dresses, swimwear, and suits, for a variety of audiences and in various types of media.

Insurance Sales Agents

Most people have their first contact with an insurance company through an insurance sales agent. Insurance agents sell policies that provide individuals and businesses with financial protection against loss. They plan for the financial security of individuals, families, and businesses; advise about insurance protection for automobiles, homes, businesses, or other property; prepare reports and maintain records; and help policyholders settle insurance claims.

Real Estate Brokers and Sales Agents

One of the most complex and important financial events in peoples' lives is the purchase or sale of a home or investment property. As a result, people usually seek the help of real estate brokers and sales agents when buying or selling real estate. Real estate brokers and sales agents have a thorough knowledge of the real estate market in their community. They know which neighborhoods will best fit clients' needs and budgets. They are familiar with local zoning and tax laws and know where to obtain financing. Agents and brokers also act as an intermediary in price negotiations between buyers and sellers.

Retail Salespersons

Whether selling shoes, computer equipment, or automobiles, retail salespersons assist customers in finding what they are looking for and try to interest them in buying the merchandise. They describe a product's features, demonstrate its use, or show

225

various models and colors. For some sales jobs, particularly those involving expensive and complex items, retail salespersons need special knowledge or skills. For example, salespersons who sell automobiles must be able to explain to customers the features of various models, warranty information, the meaning of manufacturers' specifications, and the types of options and financing available.

Sales Engineers

Many products and services are highly complex. Sales engineers, using their engineering skills, help customers determine which products or services provided by the sales engineer's employer best suit their needs. Sales engineers—who also may be called *manufacturers' agents*, *sales representatives*, or *technical sales support workers*—often work with both the customer and the production, engineering, or research and development departments of their company to determine how products and services could be designed or modified to best suit the customer's needs.

Sales Representatives, Wholesale and Manufacturing

Sales representatives are an important part of manufacturers' and wholesalers' success. Their primary duties are to interest wholesale and retail buyers and purchasing agents in their merchandise and to address any of the client's questions or concerns. Sales representatives represent one or several manufacturers or wholesale distributors by selling one product or a complementary line of products. Depending on where they work, sales representatives have different job titles. Those employed directly by a manufacturer or wholesaler are often called *sales representatives*. *Manufacturers' agents* or *manufacturers' representatives* are self-employed sales workers who contract their services to all types of manufacturing companies. However, many of these titles are used interchangeably.

Sales Worker Supervisors

Sales worker supervisors oversee the work of sales and related workers. They are responsible for interviewing, hiring, and training employees, as well as preparing work schedules and assigning workers to specific duties. Many of these workers hold job titles such as *sales manager* or *department manager*. Workers with the title *manager*, who mainly supervise sales associates and other frontline workers, are called supervisors rather than managers in the *Handbook,* even though many of these workers often perform many managerial functions.

Securities, Commodities, and Financial Services Sales Agents

Most investors, whether they are individuals with a few hundred dollars to invest or large institutions with millions, use securities, commodities, and financial services sales agents when buying or selling stocks, bonds, shares in mutual funds, insurance annuities, or other financial products. In addition, many clients seek out these agents for advice on investments, estate planning, and other financial matters. The most important part of a sales agent's job is finding clients and building a customer base.

Travel Agents

Constantly changing airfares and schedules, thousands of available vacation packages, and a vast amount of travel information on the Internet can make travel planning frustrating and time-consuming. To sort out the many travel options, tourists and businesspeople often turn to travel agents, who assess their needs and help them make the best possible travel arrangements. Also, many major cruise lines, resorts, and specialty travel groups use travel agents to promote travel packages to millions of people every year.

ADMINISTRATIVE SUPPORT

Administrative support occupations can be found in virtually all industries. Workers in this group prepare and keep records; operate office machines; arrange schedules and reservations; collect, distribute, or account for money, material, mail, or messages; or perform similar administrative duties.

The nature of these occupations is changing as a result of computer technology. From word processors in business offices to optical scanners in post offices to computerized reservation systems in airports, these new machines have raised workers' productivity and have led to faster and more efficient services. Changes in the office environment are expected to continue. This has produced a demand for workers who are able to cope with change and adapt to new technologies.

Administrative support occupations require workers with good basic skills. Workers must understand what they read, know spelling and grammar, and do arithmetic correctly. Keying skills and the ability to prepare neat, accurate paperwork are required for nearly all entry-level positions. For occupations such as bank clerk, bookkeeper, collection worker, and statistical clerk, an ability to work with numbers is particularly important. Bank teller, hotel clerk, receptionist, reservation and passenger agent, and similar occupations require constant contact with customers, so workers must be pleasant, tactful, and outgoing. The following occupations are included in the Administrative Support group.

Communications Equipment Operators

Most communications equipment operators work as *switchboard operators* for a wide variety of businesses, such as hospitals, hotels, and personnel-supply services. They also may handle other clerical duties, such as providing information, taking messages, and announcing visitors. Technological improvements have automated many of the tasks handled by switchboard operators. Some communications equipment operators work as *telephone operators*, assisting customers in making telephone calls.

Computer Operators

Computer operators oversee the operation of computer hardware systems, ensuring that these machines are used as efficiently as possible. Computer operators must anticipate problems and take preventive action, as well as solve problems that occur during operations. The duties of computer operators vary with the size of the installation, the type of equipment used, and the policies of the employer. Generally, operators control the console of either a mainframe digital computer or a group of minicomputers.

Court Reporters

Court reporters typically take verbatim reports of speeches, conversations, legal proceedings, meetings, and other events when written accounts of spoken words are necessary. They are responsible for ensuring a complete, accurate, and secure legal record. In addition to preparing and protecting the legal record, many court reporters assist judges and trial attorneys in a variety of ways, such as organizing and searching for information in the official record or making suggestions regarding courtroom administration and procedure.

Data Entry and Information Processing Workers

Organizations need to process a rapidly growing amount of information. Data entry and information processing workers help ensure this work is handled smoothly and efficiently. By keying text, entering data into a computer, operating a variety of office machines, and performing other clerical duties, these workers help organizations keep up with the rapid changes of the Information Age.

Desktop Publishers

Using desktop publishing or word processing software, desktop publishers format text and combine it with photographs, charts, and other visual elements to create publication-ready material. Materials produced by desktop publishers include books, business cards, calendars, magazines, newsletters, newspapers, packaging, slides, and tickets. As companies have brought the production of marketing, promotional, and other kinds of materials in-house, they increasingly have employed people who can produce such materials.

Financial Clerks

Financial clerks keep track of money. They record all amounts coming into or leaving an organization. Their records are vital to an organization's need to keep track of all revenues and expenses. While most financial clerks work in offices, maintaining and processing various accounting records, some deal directly with customers, taking in and paying out money. When bills are not paid on time, financial clerks must contact customers to find out why and to attempt to resolve the problem. Other clerks keep track of a store's inventory and order replacement stock when supplies are low. Specific occupational titles include *bill and account collectors*; *billing and posting clerks and machine operators*; *bookkeeping, accounting, and auditing clerks*; *gaming cage workers*; *payroll and timekeeping clerks*; *procurement clerks*; and *tellers*.

Information and Record Clerks

Information and record clerks are found in nearly every industry in the nation, gathering data and providing information to the public. The specific duties of these clerks vary as widely as the job titles they hold. Although their day-to-day duties vary widely, most information clerks greet customers, guests, or other visitors. Many also answer telephones and either obtain information from or provide information to the public. Most information clerks use multiline telephones, fax machines, and personal computers. Sample occupations include *brokerage clerks*; *customer service representatives*; *hotel, motel, and resort desk clerks*; *interviewers*; *order clerks*; *receptionists*; and *reservation and transportation ticket agents and travel clerks*.

Material Recording, Scheduling, Dispatching, and Distributing

Workers in this group are responsible for a variety of communications, record keeping, and scheduling operations. Typically, they coordinate, expedite, and track orders for personnel, materials, and equipment. *Cargo and freight agents* route and track cargo and freight shipments from airline, train, or truck terminals or shipping docks. *Couriers and messengers* deliver letters, important business documents, or packages within a firm, to other businesses, or to customers. *Dispatchers* receive requests for service and initiate action to provide that service. *Meter readers* read meters and record consumption of electricity, gas, water, or steam. *Shipping, receiving, and traffic clerks* track all incoming and outgoing shipments of goods transferred between businesses, suppliers, and customers. *Stock clerks and order fillers* receive, unpack, and store materials and equipment and maintain and distribute inventories.

Office and Administrative Support Worker Supervisors and Managers

All organizations need timely and effective office and administrative support to operate efficiently. Office and administrative support supervisors and managers coordinate this support. Planning the work of staff and supervising them are key functions of this job. After allocating work assignments, supervisors oversee the work to ensure that it is on schedule and meets quality standards. These workers are employed in virtually every sector of the economy, working in positions as varied as *customer services manager*, *teller supervisor*, and *shipping-and-receiving supervisor*.

Office Clerks, General

Rather than consisting of a single specialized task, the daily responsibilities of general office clerks vary depending on the specific job and the employer. Whereas some clerks spend their days filing or keying, others enter data at a computer terminal. Office clerks can also be called upon to operate photocopiers, fax machines, and other office equipment; prepare mailings; proofread copy; and answer telephones and deliver messages.

Postal Service Workers

Each week, the U.S. Postal Service delivers billions of pieces of mail, including letters, bills, advertisements, and packages. Most Postal Service workers are postal clerks or mail carriers. *Postal clerks* include a wide variety of workers such as window clerks, distribution clerks, and mail processors. *Window clerks* wait on customers at post offices, whereas *distribution clerks* and *mail processors* sort mail. *Mail carriers* deliver mail to urban and rural residences and businesses throughout the United States.

Secretaries and Administrative Assistants

As technology continues to expand in offices across the nation, the role of the office professional has greatly evolved. Office automation and organizational restructuring have led secretaries and administrative assistants to assume a wider range of new responsibilities once reserved for managerial and professional staff. Many secretaries and administrative assistants now provide training and orientation for new staff, conduct research on the Internet, and operate and troubleshoot new office technologies. In the midst of these changes, however, their core responsibilities have remained much the same, though carried out electronically rather than manually—performing and coordinating an office's administrative activities and storing, retrieving, and integrating information for dissemination to staff and clients.

Mechanical

Everyone has been frustrated by an automobile, television, or other piece of equipment that does not operate properly. Sooner or later, all machines and equipment with mechanical or electrical parts require service or repair. Occupations in the mechanical cluster include workers who install, service, and repair various types of machines and equipment and those who operate transportation equipment.

Transportation is one of the most important industries in our economy. Whenever transportation is disrupted by bad weather, disasters such as earthquakes, or labor strikes, the effects are felt immediately. Some workers in this cluster operate the transportation equipment that hauls goods and transports passengers.

Most mechanical occupations require an interest in working with tools and equipment and an ability to understand how machines work. This ability is often called mechanical aptitude. Mechanical workers often work alone and set their own schedule, but they have to get the work done correctly and on time. Patience is a requirement for many occupations. It may take hours or even days to find and fix a problem in a machine.

Mechanical workers often have to deal with customers who are upset because their machines do not work or their travel or shipping schedule has been delayed. Even though they may work under pressure, many mechanical workers enjoy working by themselves and receive satisfaction from solving mechanical problems. The Mechanical cluster includes occupations organized into two groups.

MECHANICS, INSTALLERS, AND REPAIRERS

In our high-tech society, machines of one type or another touch almost all aspects of our lives. Machines, including robots, produce our goods. Transportation equipment carries both goods and passengers throughout the world. Telephones and other communications equipment convey information quickly and efficiently. Appliances make our household chores easier. Mechanics, installers, and repairers install, maintain, and repair these and many other types of machines we rely upon.

Mechanics, installers, and repairers work in all industries. The largest proportion of such workers are employed in manufacturing plants that produce steel, automobiles, aircraft, and other durable goods. About an equal number of workers are employed in retail trade. These are firms that sell and service automobiles, household appliances, farm implements, and other mechanical equipment. A smaller proportion work in shops that service machines of all types. Most of the remaining workers in this group are employed in the transportation, construction, and public utilities industries and in all levels of government. The following occupations are included in the Mechanics, Installers, and Repairers group.

Aircraft and Avionics Equipment Mechanics and Service Technicians

To keep aircraft in peak operating condition, aircraft and avionics equipment mechanics and service technicians perform scheduled maintenance, complete inspections, and make necessary repairs. Some mechanics work on one or many different types of aircraft. Others specialize in one section of a particular type of aircraft. *Powerplant mechanics* are authorized to work on engines and do limited work on propellers. *Airframe mechanics* are authorized to work on any part of the aircraft except the instruments, powerplants, and propellers. *Combination airframe-and-powerplant mechanics* work on all parts of the plane, except instruments. *Avionics technicians* repair and maintain components used for aircraft navigation and radio communications, weather radar systems, and other instruments and computers.

Automotive Body and Related Repairers

Thousands of motor vehicles are damaged in traffic accidents every day. Although some are junked, most can be made to look and drive like new. *Automotive body repairers* straighten bent bodies, remove dents, and replace crumpled parts that are beyond repair. Usually, they can fix all types of vehicles, but most body repairers work on cars and small trucks. Some body repairers specialize in installing glass in automobiles and other vehicles. *Automotive glass installers and repairers* remove broken, cracked, or pitted windshields and window glass.

Automotive Service Technicians and Mechanics

Automotive service technicians and mechanics repair and service automobiles and light trucks. Anyone whose vehicle has broken down knows the importance of the mechanic's job. Once the cause of the problem is found, mechanics make adjustments or repairs. If a part is damaged, it is fixed or replaced. During routine service, mechanics inspect, lubricate, and adjust engines and other components. Often they repair or replace parts before they cause breakdowns. The work of automotive service technicians and mechanics has evolved from being simply mechanical to involving sophisticated technology. Automotive service technicians have developed into diagnostic, high-tech problem solvers.

Coin, Vending, and Amusement Machine Servicers and Repairers

Coin, vending, and amusement machines are a familiar sight in offices, convenience stores, arcades, and other types of businesses. These coin-operated machines give out change, dispense refreshments, and provide entertainment. Coin, vending, and amusement machine servicers and repairers install, service, and stock these machines and keep them in good working order.

Computer, Automated Teller, and Office Machine Repairers

Computer repairers, also known as *data processing equipment repairers*, service mainframes (large computers), servers (computers that manage network resources), and personal computers; printers; and disk drives. These workers primarily perform hands-on repair, maintenance, and installation of computers and related equipment. Automated teller machines (ATMs) allow customers to carry out bank transactions without the assistance of a teller. ATMs now provide a growing variety of other services, including stamp, phone card, and ticket sales. *Automated teller machine servicers* repair and service these machines. *Office machine and cash register servicers* work on photocopiers, cash registers, mail processing equipment, and fax machines.

Diesel Service Technicians and Mechanics

The diesel engine is the workhorse powering the nation's trucks and buses, because it delivers more power and is more durable than its gasoline-burning counterpart. Diesel-powered engines also are becoming more prevalent in light vehicles, including pickups and other work trucks. Diesel service technicians and mechanics, also known as *bus* and *truck mechanics* and *diesel engine specialists*, repair and maintain the diesel engines that power transportation equipment such as heavy trucks, buses, and locomotives.

Electrical and Electronics Installers and Repairers

Businesses and other organizations depend on complex electronic equipment for a variety of functions. Industrial controls automatically monitor and direct production processes on the factory floor. Transmitters and antennae provide communications links for many organizations. Electric power companies use electronic equipment to operate and control generating plants, substations, and monitoring equipment. The federal government uses radar and missile control systems to provide for the national defense and to direct commercial air traffic. These complex pieces of electronic equipment are installed, maintained, and repaired by electrical and electronics installers and repairers.

Electronic Home Entertainment Equipment Installers and Repairers

Electronic home entertainment equipment installers and repairers, also called *service technicians,* repair a variety of equipment, including televisions and radios, stereo components, video and audio disc players, video cameras, and videocassette recorders. They also repair home security systems, intercom equipment, and home theater equipment, which consists of large-screen televisions and sophisticated, surround-sound systems.

Elevator Installers and Repairers

Elevator installers and repairers—also called *elevator constructors* or *elevator mechanics*—assemble, install, and replace elevators, escalators, dumbwaiters, moving walkways, and similar equipment in new and old buildings. Once the equipment is in service, they maintain and repair it as well. They also are responsible for modernizing older equipment.

Heating, Air-Conditioning, and Refrigeration Mechanics and Installers

People always have sought ways to make their environment more comfortable. Today, heating and air-conditioning systems control the temperature, humidity, and total air quality in residential, commercial, industrial, and other buildings. In addition, refrigeration systems make it possible to store and transport food, medicine, and other perishable items. Heating, air-conditioning, and refrigeration mechanics and installers—also called *technicians*—install, maintain, and repair such systems.

Heavy Vehicle and Mobile Equipment Service Technicians and Mechanics

Heavy vehicles and mobile equipment are indispensable to many industrial activities, from construction to railroad operation. Various types of equipment move materials, till land, lift beams, and dig earth to pave the way for development and production. Heavy vehicle and mobile equipment service technicians and mechanics repair and maintain engines and hydraulic, transmission, and electrical systems powering farm equipment, cranes, bulldozers, and railcars.

Home Appliance Repairers

Anyone whose washer, dryer, or refrigerator has ever broken down knows the importance of a dependable repairer. Home appliance repairers, often called *service technicians*, keep home appliances working and help prevent breakdowns. Some repairers work specifically on small appliances such as microwaves and vacuum cleaners; others specialize in major appliances such as refrigerators, dishwashers, washers, and dryers.

Industrial Machinery Installation, Repair, and Maintenance Workers

When production workers encounter problems with the machines they operate, they call industrial machinery installation, repair, and maintenance workers. These workers include *industrial machinery mechanics*, *millwrights*, and *general maintenance and repair* and *machinery maintenance workers*. Their work is important not only because an idle machine will delay production, but also because a machine that is not properly repaired and maintained may damage the final product or injure the operator.

Line Installers and Repairers

Vast networks of wires and cables provide customers with electrical power and communications services. Networks of electrical power lines deliver electricity from generating plants to customers. Communications networks of telephone and cable television lines provide voice, video, and other communications services. These networks are constructed and maintained by line installers and repairers.

Precision Instrument and Equipment Repairers

Repairing and maintaining watches, cameras, musical instruments, medical equipment, and other precision instruments requires a high level of skill and attention to detail. For example, some devices contain tiny gears that must be manufactured to within 1/100 millimeter of design specifications, and other devices contain sophisticated electronic controls. Precision instrument and equipment repairers perform this type of exacting work.

Radio and Telecommunications Equipment Installers and Repairers

Telephones and radios depend on a variety of equipment to transmit communications signals. Electronic switches route telephone signals to their destinations. Switchboards direct telephone calls within a single location or organization. Radio transmitters and receivers relay signals from wireless phones and radios to their destinations. Newer telecommunications equipment is computerized and can communicate a variety of information, including data, graphics, and video. The workers who set up and maintain this sophisticated equipment are radio and telecommunications equipment installers and repairers.

Small Engine Mechanics

The smaller engines that power motorcycles, boats, and lawn and garden equipment have many things in common with auto and truck engines, including breakdowns. Small engine mechanics repair and service this equipment. Small engines require periodic servicing to minimize the possibility of breakdowns and to operate at peak efficiency. When breakdowns occur, small engine mechanics diagnose the cause and repair or replace the faulty parts.

TRANSPORTATION OCCUPATIONS

The majority of workers in transportation occupations operate transportation equipment such as taxicabs, limousines, trucks, buses, trains, and ships. Others operate industrial material moving equipment such as cranes, power shovels, graders, and industrial trucks. Although these occupations are found in all industries, they are concentrated in the transportation industry.

The ability to understand and follow complex operating rules, procedures, and instructions is an important requirement for most of these occupations. Bus drivers, for example, must adhere to detailed schedules, routes, and operating procedures. When operating equipment, they follow procedures to ensure the safety of people and property. The following occupations are included in the Transportation Occupations group.

Bus Drivers

Millions of Americans every day leave the driving to bus drivers. Bus drivers are essential in providing passengers with an alternative to their automobiles or other forms of transportation. *Intercity bus drivers* transport people between regions of a state or of the country; *local transit bus drivers*, within a metropolitan area or county; *motor coach drivers*, on charter excursions and tours; and *school bus drivers*, to and from schools and school-related events.

Material Moving Occupations

Workers in material moving occupations use machinery to move construction materials and other manufactured goods, earth, logs, petroleum products, grain, coal, and other heavy materials. Those who operate bulldozers, cranes, loaders, and similar equipment are often called *construction equipment operators*. Others operate industrial trucks and tractors and similar equipment in manufacturing plants and warehouses. Some operate mechanical booms and tower and cable equipment.

Rail Transportation Occupations

Rail transportation workers facilitate the movement of passengers and cargo by trains, subways, and streetcars. *Locomotive engineers* transport cargo and passengers between stations, while *rail yard engineers* move cars within yards to assemble or disassemble trains. *Subway operators* guide subway trains that transport passengers throughout a city and its suburbs. *Streetcar operators* drive electric-powered streetcars to transport passengers.

Taxi Drivers and Chauffeurs

Taxi drivers and chauffeurs pick up people and drive them to their destinations. *Taxi drivers* drive automobiles modified for transporting passengers (taxicabs). They take passengers to such places as airports, convention centers, hotels, and places of entertainment. Drivers collect fees from passengers based on the number of miles traveled or the amount of time spent reaching the destination. *Chauffeurs* drive passengers in private automobiles, limousines, or vans owned by limousine companies.

Truck Drivers and Driver/Sales Workers

Nearly all goods are transported by truck during some of the journey from producers to consumers. Goods may also be shipped between terminals or warehouses in different cities by train, ship, or plane. *Truck drivers* usually make the initial pickup from factories, consolidate cargo at terminals for intercity shipment, and deliver goods from terminals to stores and homes. Some local truck drivers have sales and customer service responsibilities. The primary responsibility of *driver/sales workers*, or *route drivers*, is to deliver and sell their firm's products over established routes or within an established territory. They sell goods such as food products (including restaurant takeout items) or pick up and deliver items such as laundry.

Water Transportation Occupations

Movement of huge amounts of cargo, as well as passengers, between nations and within our nation depends on workers in water transportation occupations. They operate and maintain deep-sea merchant ships, tugboats, towboats, ferries, dredges, excursion vessels, and other waterborne craft on the oceans, the Great Lakes, rivers and canals, and other waterways and in harbors. *Captains* or *masters* are in overall command of the operation of a vessel, and they supervise the work of any other officers and crew.

Construction

Construction workers build and remodel houses, factories, offices, stores, schools, and other structures. As a result, these occupations are often referred to as the building trades.

Construction requires a team effort. Much of the work in construction takes place one step at a time. Almost every step depends on another having been completed. Concrete masons cannot pour the foundation, for example, until the site has been cleared, trenches for footings have been dug, and forms have been set. Carpenters cannot begin framing the walls until the foundation is in place. Sheetrock cannot be nailed on walls until utilities have been installed, and so on.

Construction work requires an interest in working with one's hands and an ability to skillfully use a variety of hand tools and power equipment. Construction work is often physically demanding. Workers do a lot of standing, stooping, bending, kneeling, stretching, and lifting. They keep moving all the time, working at a steady rate. Construction workers have to be prepared to work in all kinds of weather conditions. During periods of bad weather, they may not work at all. Construction work is often very demanding, but it can be very rewarding to build something with your own hands. The following occupations are included in the Construction cluster.

Brickmasons, Blockmasons, and Stonemasons

Brickmasons, blockmasons, and stonemasons work in closely related trades creating attractive, durable surfaces and structures. *Brickmasons* and *blockmasons*—who often are referred to simply as *bricklayers*—build and repair walls, floors, partitions, fireplaces, chimneys, and other structures with brick, precast masonry panels, concrete block, and other masonry materials. *Stonemasons* build stone walls, as well as set stone exteriors and floors. They work with both natural cut and artificial stone. Stonemasons usually work on nonresidential structures, such as hotels and office buildings.

Carpenters

Carpenters are involved in many different kinds of construction activity. They cut, fit, and assemble wood and other materials in the construction of buildings, highways, bridges, docks, industrial plants, and many other structures. The duties of carpenters vary by type of employer. A carpenter employed by a special trade contractor, for example, may specialize in setting forms for concrete construction. One who is employed by a general building contractor, however, may frame walls and partitions, fit doors and windows, and install kitchen cabinets.

Carpet, Floor, and Tile Installers and Finishers

Carpet, tile, and other types of floor coverings not only serve an important basic function in buildings but also enhance their appearance. Carpet, floor, and tile installers and finishers lay these floor coverings in homes, offices, hospitals, stores, restaurants, and many other types of buildings. Tile also is installed on walls and ceilings.

Cement Masons, Concrete Finishers, Segmental Pavers, and Terrazzo Workers

Cement masons, concrete finishers, and terrazzo workers all work with concrete, one of the most common and durable materials used in construc-tion. Once set, concrete becomes the foundation for everything from decorative patios and floors to huge dams or miles of roadways. *Cement masons* and *concrete finishers* place and finish the concrete. *Segmental pavers* lay out, cut, and install pavers, which are flat pieces of masonry usually made from compacted concrete or brick. *Terrazzo workers* create attractive walkways, floors, patios, and panels by setting a layer of marble chips and other fine aggregates on the surface of finished concrete.

Construction Equipment Operators

Construction equipment operators use machinery to move construction materials, earth, and other heavy materials and to apply asphalt and concrete to roads and other structures. Operators control equipment by moving levers or foot pedals, operating switches, or turning dials. The operation of much of this equipment is becoming more complex as a result of computerized controls. Construction equipment operators may also set up and inspect equipment, make adjustments, and perform minor repairs.

Construction Laborers

Construction laborers perform a wide range of physically demanding tasks involving building and highway construction, tunnel and shaft excavation, hazardous waste removal, and demolition. Although the term *laborer* implies work that requires relatively little skill or training, many tasks that these workers perform require a fairly high level of training and experience. Construction laborers may sometimes help other craft workers, including carpenters, plasterers, and masons.

Drywall Installers, Ceiling Tile Installers, and Tapers

Drywall consists of a rigid, thin layer of gypsum between two layers of heavy paper. It is used for walls and ceilings in most buildings today. There are two kinds of drywall workers—*installers* and *tapers*—although many workers do both types of work. Installers fasten drywall panels to the inside framework of residential houses and other buildings. Tapers, or finishers, prepare these panels for painting by taping and finishing joints and imperfections. *Ceiling tile installers* apply or mount acoustical tiles or blocks, strips, or sheets of shock-absorbing materials to ceilings and walls of buildings to reduce reflection of sound or to decorate rooms.

Electricians

Electricians install and maintain electrical systems for a variety of purposes, including climate control, security, and communications. They also may install and maintain the electronic controls for machines in business and industry. Electricians may install cable for telephones, computers, and other telecommunications and electronic equipment. They also may connect motors to electrical power and install electronic controls for industrial equipment.

Glaziers

Glass serves many uses in modern buildings. Glaziers select, cut, install, replace, and remove all types of glass, as well as plastics and similar materials used as glass substitutes. In residential work, glaziers replace glass in windows; install mirrors, shower doors, and bathtub enclosures; and fit glass for tabletops and display cases. In commercial construction, glaziers are involved in the installation of large glass storefront windows for supermarkets, banks, auto dealerships, and similar establishments. Glass panels are also used for doors, office dividers, and skylights. In the construction of large commercial buildings, glaziers build metal framework extrusions and install glass panels or curtain walls.

Hazardous Materials Removal Workers

Increased public awareness and federal and state regulations are resulting in the removal of hazardous materials from buildings, facilities, and the environment to promote public health and safety. Hazardous materials removal workers identify, remove, package, transport, and dispose of various hazardous materials, including asbestos, lead, and radioactive and nuclear materials. The removal of hazardous materials, or "hazmats," from public places and the environment also is called abatement, remediation, and decontamination.

Insulation Workers

Properly insulated buildings reduce energy consumption by keeping heat in during the winter and out in the summer. Meat storage rooms, vats, tanks, vessels, boilers, and steam pipes also are insulated to prevent the wasteful transfer of heat. Insulation workers install this insulating material. Insulation workers cement, staple, wire, tape, or spray insulation.

Painters and Paperhangers

Paint and wall coverings make surfaces more attractive and bright. Although some people do both painting and paperhanging, each requires different skills. Painters apply paint, stain, varnish, and other finishes to buildings and other structures. Paperhangers cover walls and ceilings with decorative wall coverings made of paper, vinyl, or fabric.

Pipelayers, Plumbers, Pipefitters, and Steamfitters

Although pipelaying, plumbing, pipefitting, and steamfitting sometimes are considered a single trade, workers generally specialize in one of the four areas. *Pipelayers* lay clay, concrete, plastic, or cast-iron pipe for drains, sewers, water mains, and oil or gas lines. *Plumbers* install and repair the water, waste disposal, drainage, and gas systems in homes and commercial and industrial buildings. Plumbers also install plumbing fixtures—bathtubs, showers, sinks, and toilets—and appliances such as dishwashers and water heaters. *Pipefitters* install and repair both high- and low-pressure pipe systems used in manufacturing, generating electricity, and heating and cooling buildings. *Steamfitters* install pipe systems that move liquids or gases under high pressure.

Plasterers and Stucco Masons

Plasterers apply plaster to interior walls and ceilings to form fire-resistant and relatively soundproof surfaces. They also apply plaster veneer over drywall to create smooth or textured abrasion-resistant finishes. In addition, plasterers install prefabricated exterior insulation systems over existing walls and cast ornamental designs in plaster. *Stucco masons* apply durable plasters, such as polymer-based acrylic finishes and stucco, to exterior surfaces.

Roofers

A leaky roof can damage ceilings, walls, and furnishings. There are two types of roofs: flat and pitched (slanted). Most commercial, industrial, and apartment buildings have flat or slightly sloping roofs. Most houses have pitched roofs. Roofers install and repair both flat and pitched roofs, although some specialize in one type.

Sheet Metal Workers

Sheet metal workers make, install, and maintain air-conditioning, heating, ventilation, and pollution control duct systems; roofs; siding; rain gutters and downspouts; skylights; restaurant equipment; outdoor signs; and many other building parts and products made from metal sheets. They may also work with fiberglass and plastic materials. Although some workers specialize in fabrication, installation, or maintenance, most do all three jobs.

Structural and Reinforcing Iron and Metal Workers

Materials made from iron, steel, aluminum, and bronze are used extensively in the construction of highways, bridges, power transmission towers, and many large buildings. Structural and reinforcing iron and metal workers fabricate, assemble, and install these products. These workers also repair, renovate, and maintain older buildings and structures.

Production

Automobiles, gasoline, newspapers, eyeglasses, electricity, blue jeans, furniture, packaged meats, and most other products have at least one thing in common: they are made by production workers. Most production workers are found in manufacturing plants. Some, however, work in settings as different as shoe repair shops, photofinishing laboratories, jewelry stores, and meat markets.

There are thousands of production occupations. In many of them, workers specialize in just one task in the mass production of a single product. A lens inserter, for example, fits lenses into eyeglass frames. In other production occupations, workers do a variety of tasks to produce many different goods. Machinists, for example, make precision metal parts for industrial machinery, completing all of the steps that are required to finish the product. Some workers perform simple, repetitive operations on large machine tools, while others such as jewelers use hand tools to do delicate work. Not all production workers turn out products, however. Some operate complex systems of boilers, generators, pumps, and valves that produce clean water or energy.

Production workers perform manual work requiring varying degrees of skill. Some do little more than start and stop a machine and watch it while it is running. Others do highly skilled work requiring a great deal of precision. Most occupations require coordination and manual dexterity. The typical production worker stands or sits at a workstation all day performing repetitive, concrete tasks. The following occupations are included in the Production cluster.

Assemblers and Fabricators

Assemblers and fabricators produce a wide range of finished goods. They produce intricate manufactured products, such as aircraft, automobile engines, computers, and electrical and electronic components. Assemblers may work on subassemblies or the final assembly of an array of finished products or components. Virtually all assemblers and fabricators work in plants that manufacture durable goods, such as computers and automobile engines. Assembly work varies from simple, repetitive jobs to those requiring great precision.

Boilermakers

Boilermakers and boilermaker mechanics construct, assemble, and repair boilers, vats, and other large vessels that hold liquids and gases. Boilers supply steam to drive huge turbines in electric power plants and to provide heat or power in buildings, factories, and ships. Tanks and vats are used to process and store chemicals, oil, beer, and hundreds of other products.

Bookbinders and Bindery Workers

The process of combining printed sheets into finished products such as books, magazines, catalogs, folders, directories, or product packaging is known as binding. Binding involves cutting, folding, gathering, gluing, stapling, stitching, trimming, sewing, wrapping, and other finishing operations. Bindery workers operate and maintain the machines that perform these various tasks.

Computer-Control Programmers and Operators

Computer-control programmers and operators use computer numerically controlled (CNC) machines to cut and shape precision products, such as automobile parts, machine parts, and compressors. Computer-control programmers and operators normally produce large quantities of one part, although they may produce small batches or one-of-a-kind items. They use their knowledge of the working properties of metals and their skill with CNC programming to design and carry out the operations needed to make machined products that meet precise specifications.

Dental Laboratory Technicians

Dental laboratory technicians fill prescriptions from dentists for crowns, bridges, dentures, and similar devices. First, dentists send a specification of the item to be fabricated, along with an impression (mold) of the patient's mouth or teeth. Based upon the dentist's specifications, technicians build and shape a wax tooth or teeth model, using small hand instruments called wax spatulas and wax carvers. They use this wax model to cast the metal framework for the device. In some laboratories, technicians perform all stages of the work, whereas in other labs, each technician does only a few. The work is extremely delicate and time-consuming.

Food Processing Occupations

Food processing occupations include many different types of workers involved in processing raw food products into finished goods ready for sale by grocers, wholesalers, restaurants, or institutional food services. These workers perform a variety of tasks and are responsible for producing many of the food products found in every household. Common occupations include *meatpackers*, *butchers*, *poultry and fish cutters and trimmers*, *bakers*, and *food batchmakers*.

Inspectors, Testers, Sorters, Samplers, and Weighers

Inspectors, testers, sorters, samplers, and weighers ensure that your food will not make you sick, your car will run properly, and your pants will not split the first time you wear them. These workers monitor or audit virtually all types of manufactured products to ensure that they meet quality standards. As quality becomes increasingly important to the success of many production firms, daily duties of inspectors have changed. In some cases, their titles also have changed, to *quality control inspector* or a similar name.

Jewelers and Precious Stone and Metal Workers

Jewelers use a variety of common and specialized hand tools to design and manufacture new pieces of jewelry; cut, set, and polish stones; and repair or adjust rings, necklaces, bracelets, earrings, and other jewelry. Jewelers usually specialize in one or more of these areas. Jewelers may work for large jewelry manufacturing firms or small retail jewelry shops or may open their own business. Regardless of the type of work done or the work setting, jewelers require a high degree of skill, precision, and attention to detail.

Machinists

Machinists use machine tools, such as lathes, milling machines, and spindles, to produce precision metal parts. Although they may produce large quantities of one part, precision machinists often produce small batches or one-of-a-kind items. They use their knowledge of the working properties of metals and their skill with machine tools to plan and carry out the operations needed to make machined products that meet precise specifications.

Machine Setters, Operators, and Tenders

Consider the parts of a toaster, such as the metal or plastic housing or the lever that lowers the toast. These parts, and many other metal and plastic products, are produced by metalworking and plastics-working machine operators. In fact, machine tool operators in the metalworking and plastics industries play a major part in producing most of the consumer products on which we rely daily. In general, these workers can be separated into two groups—those who set up machines for operation and those who tend the machines during production.

Ophthalmic Laboratory Technicians

Ophthalmic laboratory technicians—also known as *manufacturing opticians*, *optical mechanics*, or *optical goods workers*—make prescription eyeglass or contact lenses. Prescription lenses are curved in such a way that light is correctly focused onto the retina of the patient's eye, improving vision. Ophthalmic laboratory technicians cut, grind, edge, and finish lenses according to specifications provided by dispensing opticians, optometrists, or ophthalmologists and may insert lenses into frames to produce finished glasses.

Painting and Coating Workers

Millions of items ranging from cars to candy are covered by paint, plastic, varnish, chocolate, or some other type of coating solution. Often the protection provided by the paint or coating is essential to the product, like the coating of insulating material covering wires and other electrical and electronic components. Many paints and coatings have dual purposes, such as the paint finish on an automobile, which heightens the visual appearance of the vehicle while providing protection from corrosion. Painting, coating, and spraying machine setters, operators, and tenders control the machinery that applies these paints and coatings to a wide range of manufactured products.

Photographic Process Workers and Processing Machine Operators

Both amateur and professional photographers rely heavily on photographic process workers and processing machine operators to develop film, make prints or slides, and do related tasks, such as enlarging or retouching photographs. *Photographic processing machine operators* operate various machines, such as mounting presses and motion picture film printing, photographic printing, and film developing machines. *Photographic process workers* perform more delicate tasks, such as retouching photographic negatives and prints to emphasize or correct specific features.

Power Plant Operators, Distributors, and Dispatchers

Electricity is vital for most everyday activities. From the moment you flip the first switch each morning, you are connecting to a huge network of people, electric lines, and generating equipment. *Power plant operators* control the machinery that generates electricity. *Power distributors* and *dispatchers* control the flow of electricity from the power plant over a network of transmission lines to industrial plants and substations and, finally, over distribution lines to residential users.

Prepress Technicians and Workers

The printing process has three stages—prepress, press, and postpress (binding). Prepress technicians and workers prepare material for printing presses. They perform a variety of tasks involved with transforming text and pictures into finished pages and making printing plates of the pages. Advances in computer software and printing technology continue to change the nature of prepress work.

Printing Machine Operators

Printing machine operators prepare, operate, and maintain the printing presses in a pressroom. Duties vary according to the type of press they operate. Operation involves running the press and maintaining the paper feeders. Throughout the run, operators must also pull sheets to check for any imperfections and make adjustments accordingly.

Semiconductor Processors

Electronic semiconductors—also known as computer chips, microchips, or integrated chips—are the miniature but powerful brains of high-tech equipment. They are composed of a myriad of tiny aluminum wires and electric switches, which manipulate the flow of electrical current. Semiconductor processors are responsible for many of the steps necessary to manufacture each semiconductor that goes into a personal computer, a missile guidance system, and a host of other electronic equipment.

Stationary Engineers and Boiler Operators

Heating, air-conditioning, and ventilation systems keep large buildings comfortable all year long. Industrial plants often have facilities to provide electrical power, steam, or other services. Stationary engineers and boiler operators control and maintain these systems, which include boilers, air-conditioning and refrigeration equipment, diesel engines, turbines, generators, pumps, condensers, and compressors. The equipment that stationary engineers and boiler operators control is similar to equipment operated by locomotive or marine engineers, except that it is not on a moving vehicle.

Textile, Apparel, and Furnishings Occupations

Textiles and leather clothe our bodies, cover our furniture, and adorn our homes. Textile, apparel, and furnishings workers produce these materials and fashion them into a wide range of products that we use in our daily lives. Jobs may employ computers, large industrial machinery, or smaller power equipment or may involve substantial handwork. Specific occupations include *textile machine operators*, *apparel workers*, *shoe and leather workers*, *upholsterers*, and *laundry and dry cleaning workers*.

Tool and Die Makers

Tool and die makers are highly skilled workers who produce tools, dies, and special guiding and holding devices that are used in manufacturing. *Toolmakers* craft precision tools that are used to cut, shape, and form metal and other materials. *Diemakers* construct metal forms (dies) that are used to shape metal in stamping and forging operations.

Water and Liquid Waste Treatment Plant and System Operators

Clean water is essential for many things, including health, recreation, fish and wildlife, and the needs of industry. *Water treatment plant and system operators* treat water so that it is safe to drink. *Liquid waste treatment plant and system operators*, also known as *wastewater treatment plant and system operators*, remove harmful pollutants from domestic and industrial liquid waste so that it is safe to return to the environment.

Welding, Soldering, and Brazing Workers

Welding is the most common way of permanently joining metal parts. In this process, heat is applied to metal pieces, melting and fusing them to form a permanent bond. Because of the strength of welded materials, welding is used in shipbuilding, automobile manufacturing and repair, aerospace applications, and thousands of other manufacturing activities. Welding also is used to join beams when constructing buildings, bridges, and other structures and to join pipes in pipelines, power plants, and refineries. Like arc welding, soldering and brazing use metal to join two pieces of metal.

Woodworkers

Woodworkers comprise a variety of occupations. Some produce the structural elements of buildings. Others mill hardwood and softwood lumber. Some assemble finished wood products. Woodworkers are found in primary industries that produce wood, such as sawmills and plywood mills, as well as in secondary industries that use wood to manufacture furniture, kitchen cabinets, musical instruments, and other fabricated wood products. Precision woodworkers are found in small shops making architectural woodwork, furniture, and other specialty items.

Natural Resources

Workers in natural resources occupations provide us with many of the raw materials that are used to satisfy our basic needs for food, shelter, and clothing. These are the growers and gatherers who depend largely on the resources of nature for their livelihood.

Agricultural workers raise plants and animals that provide us with food and fiber (such as wool and cotton). Forestry workers harvest trees that provide lumber for building and furniture construction as well as pulp for a variety of paper products. Fishers gather marine and animal life that is eaten and used in fertilizer and other products. Extractive workers mine the fuels and other raw materials needed for heat and power and used in manufacturing, construction, and agriculture.

Workers in natural resources occupations have an interest in nature and the environment around them. They enjoy working outdoors. Many workers are their own bosses or work with little or no supervision. Natural resources workers should have a strong sense of responsibility and a commitment to the long-term protection and improvement of the environment. The following occupations are included in the Natural Resources cluster.

Agricultural Workers

Agricultural workers have a range of responsibilities, from planting, cultivating, grading, and sorting agricultural products to inspecting agricultural commodities and facilities. They may work with food crops, animals, or trees, shrubs, and other plants. Depending on their jobs, they may work outdoors or indoors. Nine out of ten agricultural workers are farm workers.

Farmers, Ranchers, and Agricultural Managers

American farmers, ranchers, and agricultural managers direct the activities of one of the world's largest and most productive agricultural sectors. They produce enough food and fiber to meet the needs of the United States, as well as a surplus for export. *Farmers* and *ranchers* may be owners or tenants who pay to use the land. The type of farm they operate (crop, livestock, or horticulture) determines the specific tasks they perform. *Agricultural managers* guide and assist farmers and ranchers in maximizing the financial returns from their land by managing the day-to-day activities.

Fishers and Fishing Vessel Operators

Fishers and fishing vessel operators catch and trap various types of marine life for human consumption, animal feed, bait, and other uses. Fishers use a variety of hand-operated equipment, such as nets and hooks, to gather finfish and shellfish, catch water animals such as frogs and turtles, and harvest marine life such as Irish moss and kelp. Historically most fishers were involved with the traditional commercial fishery. Today, some captains and deckhands are primarily employed in support of the sport or recreational fishery.

Forest, Conservation, and Logging Workers

The nation's forests are a rich natural resource, providing beauty and tranquility, varied recreational areas, and wood for commercial use. Managing forests and woodlands requires many different kinds of workers. Forest and conservation workers help develop, maintain, and protect these forests by growing and planting new tree seedlings, fighting insects and diseases that attack trees, and helping to control soil erosion. Timber cutting and logging workers harvest thousands of acres of forests each year for the timber that provides the raw material for countless consumer and industrial products.

Military

The mission of the U.S. Armed Forces is to deter aggression and defend the nation in times of conflict. The Army prepares for land-based defense, while the Air Force provides for air and space defense. The Navy organizes and trains forces primarily for sea defense, while the Marine Corps, part of the Department of the Navy, prepares for land invasion in support of naval or amphibious operations. The Coast Guard, under the Department of Transportation (except in wartime, when it serves with the Navy), enforces federal maritime laws, rescues distressed vessels and aircraft at sea, operates aids to navigation, and prevents smuggling.

Together, the Armed Forces constitute America's largest employer. There are more than 2,000 basic and advanced military occupational specialties for enlisted personnel and 1,600 for officers. The occupations are organized into the following 15 broad groups. Some groups are limited to officers (O), some are limited to enlisted personnel (E), and some groups include both enlisted personnel and officers (E, O).

- Executive, Administrative, and Managerial (O)
- Human Services (E, O)
- Media and Public Affairs (E, O)
- Health Diagnosing and Treating Practitioner (O)
- Health Care (E, O)
- Engineering, Science, and Technical (E, O)
- Administrative (E)
- Service (E)
- Vehicle and Machinery Mechanic (E)
- Electronic and Electrical Equipment Repair (E)
- Construction (E)
- Machine Operator and Precision Work (E)
- Transportation (O)
- Transportation and Material Handling (E)
- Combat Specialty (E, O)

About 75 percent of these occupations involve duties that are basically the same as those in occupations in the civilian sector. Note how similar these military occupational groups are to the 11 civilian occupational clusters that have been described in previous sections of this workbook.

About 25 percent of military occupations, however, are unique to the Armed Forces. These are primarily the combat specialty occupations that are concerned with direct military operations. Military occupations are divided into military enlisted occupations and military officer occupations.

Enlisted personnel are the workers and supervisors who carry out and maintain the basic operations of the military. Their roles are like those of company employees or supervisors. They are usually high school graduates and are required to meet minimum physical and aptitude standards before enlisting.

Officers are the leaders of the military and usually are college graduates. Officers develop plans, set objectives, and lead other officers and enlisted personnel in attaining their goals. Young men and women hoping to become officers must meet the minimum entrance requirements set by each military service. A brief discussion of Combat Specialty occupations follows.

COMBAT SPECIALTY OCCUPATIONS/ ENLISTED PERSONNEL

These are the fighting forces of the military. In the event of war, these are the personnel who directly engage the enemy in battle. Five specialties constitute this group.

Artillery Crew Members

Artillery includes weapons that fire large shells or missiles. The military uses artillery to support infantry and tank units in combat. Artillery is also used to protect land and sea forces from air attack. Artillery crew members position, direct, and fire artillery guns, cannons, howitzers, missiles, and rockets to destroy enemy positions and aircraft.

Combat Engineers

Combat situations often require rapid travel across difficult terrain and swift-flowing rivers. Combat engineers construct trails, roads, and temporary shelters and erect floating or prefabricated bridges. They lay and clear minefields, construct field fortifications such as bunkers and gun emplacements, and perform other field construction duties. This is the only specialty in this group open to women.

Infantrymen

The infantry is the main land combat force of the military. In peacetime, the infantry's role is to stay ready to defend the country. In combat, the role of the infantry is to capture or destroy enemy ground forces and repel enemy attacks. Infantrymen operate weapons and equipment to engage and destroy enemy ground forces.

Special Operations Forces

When the military has difficult and dangerous missions to perform, it calls upon special operations teams. These elite combat forces stay in a constant state of readiness to strike anywhere in the world on a moment's notice. Special operations forces team members conduct offensive raids, demolitions, intelligence, search and rescue, and other missions from aboard aircraft, helicopters, ships, or submarines.

Tank Crew Members

In peacetime, the role of tank and armor units is to stay ready to defend national security anywhere in the world. In combat, their role is to engage and destroy the enemy. Tanks also conduct scouting missions and support infantry units during combat. Tank crew members work as a team to operate armored equipment and fire weapons to destroy enemy positions.

COMBAT SPECIALTY OCCUPATIONS/ OFFICERS

Military officers train and direct the activities of fighting forces. Officers serve their country daily, sometimes placing themselves in danger. They are responsible for the well-being, training, and readiness of the people they lead. Five specialties constitute this group.

Artillery Officers

The military uses artillery to support infantry and tank units in combat and to protect land and sea forces from air attack. Artillery officers direct artillery crewmembers as they position, maintain, and fire guns, cannons, howitzers, and rockets at enemy positions. They normally specialize by type of artillery. There are women artillery officers, but some specialties in this occupation are open only to men.

Infantry Officers

In combat, the infantry is deployed to capture or destroy enemy forces on the ground and to repel enemy invasions. Infantry officers direct, train, and lead infantry units. Infantry officers may specialize in amphibious warfare (attacking land from the water), airborne operations (parachuting into battle), special operations, or Ranger operations (special units skilled in combat in many different geographic areas).

Missile System Officers

Ballistic missiles are powerful weapons that travel thousands of miles to their targets. They are fired from underground silos, submarines, and land-based launchers. Missile system officers direct missile crews as they target, launch, test, and maintain ballistic missiles. This occupation is open to women as well as men.

Special Operations Officers

Each service has specially trained forces to perform rapid strike missions. These elite forces must be prepared to strike anywhere at any time. Special operations officers lead special operations forces in offensive raids, demolitions, intelligence gathering, search and rescue, and other missions.

Tank Officers

In combat, tank and armor units operate tanks, armored vehicles, and amphibious assault vehicles to engage and destroy the enemy. Tank officers lead tank and armor units. They normally specialize by type of tank unit, such as armor, cavalry, or amphibious assault.

OCCUPATIONAL SEARCH FORM

TITLE OF THE OCCUPATION _____

NATURE OF THE WORK

List five major tasks that workers in this occupation perform.

1. _____

_____

2. _____

_____

3. _____

_____

4. _____

_____

5. _____

_____

WORKING CONDITIONS

Write down the normal working hours, if they are listed. _____

_____

Describe the typical working conditions. _____

_____

_____

Are there any unpleasant or dangerous aspects to this occupation? _____

_____

EMPLOYMENT

Number of jobs in the occupation _____ Year provided _____

In what types of industries or locations do people in this occupation work?

_____

TRAINING, OTHER QUALIFICATIONS, AND ADVANCEMENT

What is the preferred or required level of education or training? _____

_____

List any licensure or certification requirements. _____

_____

List any special abilities or qualifications recommended or required. _____

_____

What opportunities are there for advancement? _____

JOB OUTLOOK

Check the statement in each column below that best describes the future outlook for this occupation.

Change in Employment	**Opportunities and Competition**
____ Faster than average growth	____ Very good to excellent opportunities
____ Average growth	____ Good opportunities
____ Slower than average growth	____ May face competition
____ Little change	____ Keen competition
____ Decline	

EARNINGS

Write down the average yearly starting salary, if available._____

Range of average yearly earnings _____ Year provided _____

RELATED OCCUPATIONS

List the titles of related occupations.

1. _____   5. _____
2. _____   6. _____
3. _____   7. _____
4. _____   8. _____

SOURCES OF ADDITIONAL INFORMATION

List names and addresses of places where further information may be obtained.

_____

_____

_____

_____

_____

_____

Source of information: *Occupational Outlook Handbook* 20__/20__ Edition, pages _____